# TOP FOOD ALLERGIES

# THE INFAMOUS -8-

## THE BIRTHDAY PARTY ADVENTURE

### by Anna Laurie

**Illustrations John McNees**

**Top Food Alergies - THE INFAMOUS 8 - Birthday Party Adventure**
**copyright © 2019 Anna M. Laurie**

Contact the author: anna@foodieqfit.com

Published by Anna M. Laurie/FoodieQFit.com.
Please visit foodieqfit.com for allergy information, allergen-free recipes, menu consultations, coaching, and more.

FOODIE Q FIT

ISBN - 13: 978-0-9994269-0-6

Illustrations copyright © 2019 held by
John McNees and NOW Illustration and Design
nowillustration@gmail.com
nowillustrationanddesign.com

# DEDICATION PAGE

This book is dedicated to my family. My husband and my children are my life and my inspiration. My three sons all have food allergies. This books is the result of my many years of cooking safely for them.

To my oldest son, Matthew, who said, "Mom, you got this." Thank you for sitting with me and helping me come up with ideas for my book. I couldn't have done it without you.

To my middle son, Jake, thank you for always being so excited when I head to the kitchen to create a new recipe. You are a great taste-tester, and I appreciate your honesty and your advice on how to make foods more enjoyable for kids.

Last but not least, to my youngest son, Donato, who has the most food allergies out of all three, thank you for being my true inspiration for writing this book. I know how you always wonder if there will be something to eat at birthday parties! Thank you for creating Peanut the Kid. I am so lucky to have such a talented child to help me create this picture.

Thank you to my wonderful husband, Matthew Sr., for supporting me every step of the way, even when I didn't think I could do it. You encouraged me through all this and believed in me even when I didn't believe in myself.

To my mother and father, thank you for always being there for me and encouraging me in every way. You are amazing parents who left Italy to start a new life in America and raise three children. Mom, you made me the cook I am today thanks to the magic in your kitchen. Love you, Mom and Dad!

I would like to thank John Valentini and the late Rudy Valentini for being great, big brothers, who watched their little sister grow to who she is today.

I also want to thank my nephews, and nieces for their encouragement, inspiration, and willingness to try my recipes.

Many thanks also to all of our friends, and especially my good friends, Danielle Thompson, and Allison Gormley. We have talked so often about me writing a book. Now I've done it. Yay!

Thanks to Ava Thompson, a sweet little girl, for letting me include her in the book.

Special thanks to my niece, Sarah Pezzulo, for creating the logo for FoodieQFit.

For all the guidance and support they have given me and my children for our health and well being, special thanks to Dr Roseanne Demanski ND, Chiropractor, Dr. Gina Carucci-Carucci and Jeannie Leitao RD.

Thanks to Danielle Ozano for editing my words to be more concise and understanding.

To all the parents out there who have children with food allergies, I really hope this book helps you better understand food allergies. It's also my hope that this book makes it easier and more enjoyable for children with food allergies to go to a birthday party and not feel left out, frustrated, or different.

And a special thanks to the illustrator John McNees, a talented and amazing person to work with who has captured my vision of these characters just the way I wanted them.

# About the Author

Anna Laurie is a trained and certified holistic health counselor, nutritionist, chef, and is a mother of three boys with food allergies. She's always been interested in learning about health and nutrition, and is proud of her educational background in that field, as well as in the fields of hospitality management, and the culinary arts.

She has studied and implemented food safety standards and has even lobbied to improve school nutrition in Washington, D.C. Anna's experience and educational background in food science, food management, food nutrition, and food safety have given her a solid foundation to build this fun, informative, and educational book upon.

Writing "The Infamous 8" has also given Anna the opportunity to share all she's learned over the years about delicious, allergen-free foods. Her recipes are easy enough for everyone to make and tasty enough for even the pickiest eaters to enjoy.

If you'd like more information on Anna or to chat with her about allergies or holistic health, please visit her FoodieQFit website at http://www.foodieqfit.com/. She loves hearing from readers, and is always happy to help maximize your health and well-being!

~ ~ ~

This book is written only as a guide to issues concerning allergies and their causes. Not everything will apply to everyone. Individual cases will vary and, as always, you should consult your doctor, dietician, or allergy specialist for specific answers to your allergy questions.

At the time of writing this book, the Infamous 8 are the top 8 food allergens recognized by FALCPA. Other foods are currently being considered for inclusion in this list of food allergens.

# Table of Contents

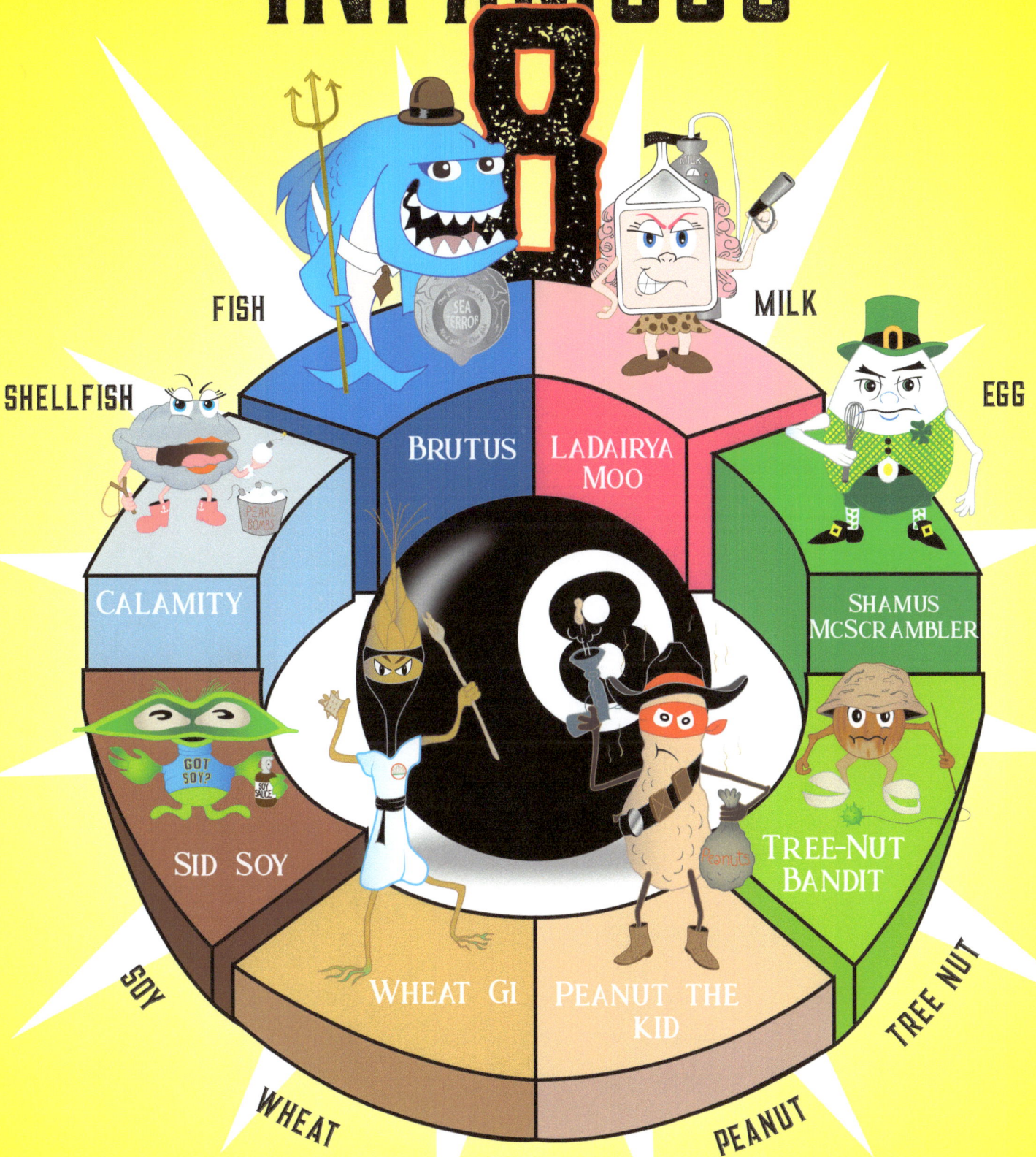

# The 8 VILLAINS

**Peanut the Kid**
NAME: aka: The Ground Nut Kid

ALLERGIES: **Peanuts:** peanut butter, ground nuts, peanut oil, goobers

OCCUPATION: Peanut Robber

WEAPON: Peanut Popper

VILLANOUS CHARACTERISTICS:
Sneaky, nutty, fights dirty and always beware of the p-nutty odor

FILE : OU812

Peanuts are also part of the Legume Gang which includes Beans, Peas and Lentiles *

* If you have a peanut allergy you should avoid legumes unless discussed with your physician

NAME: Wheat-Gi
aka: Wheat Ninja

ALLERGY: **Wheat:** bread, flour, cakes, cookies, donuts, cupcakes, and gluten.

OCCUPATION: Farmer by day, Wheat-Gi by night

WEAPON: Wheat staff
Wheat cracker stars

VILLAINOUS CHARACTERISTICS:
He loves to hide in breads and baked goods.

*Wheat is different than a Gluten intolerance or celiac disease (see chart on page 15) Gluten is a protein found in wheat, barley and rye.

FILE : YRUB4-ME

NAME: Brutus aka: Mr. Blue

ALLERGY: **Fish:** salmon, cod, pollock, tuna, tilapia, mackerel, fish oil

OCCUPATION: Sea Terror

WEAPON: Trident

VILLAINOUS CHARACTERISTICS:

He is hard to catch.

Also in Caesar Salad
Anchovies
Worchestershire sauce
Marshmallows

Beware
Fish gelatin may be hidden in hot dogs, deli meats, and fruit juice drinks

FILE : IC-12

---

NAME: LaDairya Moo

ALLERGY: Milk, butter, ice cream, sherbert, puddings, whipped cream, cream cheese, custards, yogurt, milk casein

OCCUPATION: Cattle Thief

WEAPON: Milk Blaster

VILLIANOUS CHARCTERISTICS:

Tries to hide dairy in everything she can.

Sneaks into baked goods, cookies, cakes, chocolate, caramel, salad dressings, and crackers

FILE : B4U-GO

| | |
|---|---|
| NAME: | Shamus McScrambler aka: none |
| ALLERGY: | **Egg:** breaded & batter-fried foods, cream pies, crepes & waffles, custards, puddings, ice cream, egg substitutes. |
| OCCUPATION: | A real "yolkster" |
| WEAPON: | Wild Whipper |

VILLAINOUS CHARACTERISTICS:
Likes to whisk himself into trouble.

Beware!
Some drinks may contain egg. For example, root beer and milkshakes

Regularly found in French Toast, omelets, eggnog, fried and baked goods.

**FILE : OGIC-M**

| | |
|---|---|
| NAME: | Tree Nut Bandit aka: Walter Nut |
| ALLERGY: | **Tree Nut:** almonds, walnuts chestnuts, pecans, cashews, brazil nuts, hazelnuts, pinenuts, pistachios |
| OCCUPATION: | Just hangs around |
| WEAPON: | Chestnut Mace |

VILLAINOUS CHARACTERISTICS:
Hangs around in bunches with sweet & salty sprinkles on them. These guys are lurking everywhere.

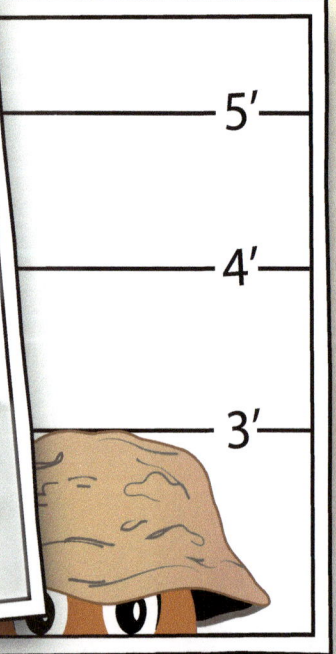

**FILE : ICUR-2**

5'

4'

3'

| | |
|---|---|
| NAME: | Calamity<br>aka: Molly Mollusk |
| ALLERGIES: | **Shell-fish:**<br>**Crustaceans:** lobster, shrimp, prawns, crayfish<br>**Mollusks:** clams, oysters, scallops, mussels |
| OCCUPATION: | Causing trouble everywhere she goes |
| WEAPON: | Pearl Bombs |

VILLANOUS CHARACTERISTICS:
Loves to sun herself on top of pizza and hides in soups and chowders.

PEARL BOMBS

HIDEOUT

**FILE : IM-MT2**

| | |
|---|---|
| NAME: | Sid Soy aka: Soy Boy |
| ALLERGY: | Soy, soy milk, soybeans, tofu, soy oil, soy flour, soy sauce, soy nuts. |
| OCCUPATION: | Shows up everywhere unexpected. Is always into something |
| WEAPON: | Soy Soaker |

VILLANOUS CHARACTERISTICS:
Looks very friendly but beware, he is in **ALMOST EVERYTHING YOU EAT,** which makes him very dangerous.

May also be found in baked goods cereal, chips candy, and chocolate

GOT SOY?

SOY SAUCE

**FILE : NE1cME**

# Our HEROES

NAME: Epi-man

SUPER POWER:
Acts fast in allergy emergencies, saves lives

OCCUPATION: Allergy superhero

WEAPON: Epinephrine

GOOD GUY

FILE : O-NO- u812

NAME: Beni-dryl

SUPER POWER:
Strikes back against Allergens - Fast relief

OCCUPATION: Epi-man's sidekick

SAYING: "You know the 'Dryl'"

GOOD GUY

FILE : T42-24T

# Food Facts

Learn more about The Infamous 8
and where they may be lurking

Throughout this section, you'll see reference numbers
below some of the descriptions (e.g. Ref. #1)
that directly relate to informational website links found in
the "Reference and Further Reading" section of this book.

# EGG ALLERGY

**Egg Allergy**- An Egg Allergy can cause life-threatening symptoms, and is commonly found in children at a very young age. This allergy is triggered when the body's immune system overreacts to proteins in egg whites or yolk. It's been stated that 70 percent of children outgrow an egg allergy by the age of 16.

*Beware – with a chicken egg allergy you also might be allergic to goose, duck, quail, and turkey eggs.*
Ref. #1

**Egg allergy affects 1.3 percent of children.**
Ref. #2

There are children who are able to eat eggs in baked goods without having an allergic reaction, but this doesn't mean the child isn't allergic to eggs. Always consult with your doctor/allergist.

**Egg Intolerance/Sensitivity** - is an inability to digest egg properly which results in digestive problems.

## SHAMUS MCSCRAMBLER: ALWAYS INTO THINGS

Eggs in all forms
Whole egg
Egg yolks
Egg substitutions
Egg whites
Dried eggs
Egg solids
Powdered eggs
Egg wash
Meringue
Mayonnaise

## HIDDEN NAMES FOUND FOR EGGS:

Albumin: egg white, dried egg whites
Ref. #3

Albumen: protein found in egg whites

Vitellin: protein found in egg yolks
Ref. #4

Globulin: protein found in egg whites

Silici albuminate: contain egg

Lysozyme: enzyme in egg white

livetin: protein found in egg yolk
Ref. #5

Simplesse: a fat substitute made from egg white protein
Ref. #6

Surimi: Japanese - a paste made from fish or meat and also contains egg whites
Ref. #7

Ovalbumin: the **main** protein found in egg whites

Ovoglobulin: medical terminology for the globulin found in egg whites

Ovomucin: a glycoprotein found in egg whites

Ovotransferrin: a glycoprotein found in egg white albumen
Ref. #8

## SHAMUS MCSCRAMBLER CAN SOMETIMES WHISK HIMSELF INTO THE LIST BELOW:

| | | | | |
|---|---|---|---|---|
| Creamy salad dressing | Caeser salad | Puddings | Baked goods | Ice cream |
| Chocolate mousse | French toast | Pancakes | Nougat | Pasta |
| Lecithin | Natural flavoring | Chocolate sauce | Icing | Chocolate |
| Souffles | Marshmallows | Breaded foods | Tartar sauce | Candy |
| Fondant | Fudge | Frostings | Fried foods | Crackers |
| Hollandaise sauce | Artificial flavoring | Pretzels | Breadcrumb | Breads |

**Some drinks that also might have egg in them:**
Wine
Coffee drinks
Milkshakes
Eggnog
Root beer
Protein shakes

**Stocks clarified with egg:** Consommé, Broth, Bouillon

**A Fish Allergy, also known as Fin Fish Allergy, can be life-threatening.** It triggers an adverse immune response, and unlike other food allergies that are present from a young age, approximately 40 percent of people don't acquire a fish allergy until adulthood. Ref. #9

Always read your labels to see if there are fish ingredients present. The most common kinds of finned fish people react to are Tuna, Salmon, and Halibut. With a fish allergy, you need to be very careful because it can become severe quickly. To be safe, avoid seafood restaurants due to cross-contamination, and understand that you can get an allergic reaction by simply smelling fish as it's being cooked! Ref. #10

Having a fish allergy doesn't mean you'll have a shellfish allergy.
Always consult your doctor/allergist to determine this.
A child who has a fish allergy must completely avoid eating it unless directed by a doctor or allergist. Make sure to always read your labels carefully.

There are Over **32,000** species of **finfish**.
I have listed some below:
Ref. #11

| | |
|---|---|
| Anchovy | Barramundi |
| Bass | Striped bass |
| White seabass | Catfish |
| Char | Arctic cod |
| Flounder | Grouper |
| Haddock | Hake |
| Halibut | Herring |
| Hoki | Lake trout |
| Lingcod | Mackerel |
| Mahi-mahi | Monkfish |
| Pollock | Perch |
| Salmon | Snapper |
| Sole | Swordfish |
| Scrod | Tilapia |
| Trout | Tuna |
| Whitefish | |

## BRUTUS IS HARD TO CATCH.
**BEWARE!** HE CAN BE HIDING IN THESE:

| | |
|---|---|
| Surimi (Imitation fish) | Worcestershire sauce |
| Bouillabaisse (fish stew) | Fish sticks |
| Caviar | Fish chowders |
| Zuppa di pesce | Cioppino |
| Bologna (may contain fish gelatin) | Hotdogs (may contain fish gelatin) |
| Fish stock | Pizza toppings (Anchovies) |
| Barbecue sauce | Fish sauce |

Caponata (Sicilian eggplant relish)
Orange juice that contains Omega-3 fatty acids = fish
Ref.#12

Some fruit juices contain fish gelatin

Fish stock Gelatin: sometimes derived from fish bones and used as an ingredient in Marshmallows.
Yogurt is also notorious for having "kosher" gelatin in it. This usually means gelatin made from fish.

## BRUTUS CAN BE SWIMMING INTO THESE THINGS TOO:

| | | | |
|---|---|---|---|
| Pet food | Pet treats | Fish oil | Omega-3 supplements |
| Fish food | Fertilizer | Cosmetics | Vitamins Soap Paint |

Ref. #13

## BOTH COME FROM THE OCEAN, BUT THEY ARE NOT "FISH":

**Agar or agar-agar:** A jelly-like substance obtained from algae (seaweed). It is used in many products, and as it comes from the ocean, you should consult your doctor/allergist to see if it's safe to use.

**Carrageenan/Irish moss:** A red marine algae found in many foods, especially in dairy products. It's used as an emulsifier, thickening agent and stabilizer. Even though it's safe for most people with a fish allergy, it would be a good idea to consult with with your doctor/allergist before consuming it. Ref. #14

# MILK ALLERGY

**BEWARE! LaDairya Moo is in here**

**A Milk or Dairy Allergy** is an adverse immune response to the protein in cow's milk and is different than having Lactose Intolerance.

**Lactose Intolerance** is an inability to digest the sugar called lactose found in ALL dairy products.

## LIST OF SOME ITEMS TO LOOK OUT FOR:

Milk
Evaporated milk
Powdered milk
Milk solids
Milk derivatives
Butter
Butter oil

Condensed milk
Buttermilk
Milk proteins
Malted milk
Dry milk
Butter fat

Ghee: clarified butter
Butter extracts
Creamers
Light cream
Cream cheese
Sherbet
Custards
Quark: a soft cheese

Butter flavorings
Butter solids
Heavy cream
Whipping cream
Ice cream
Yogurt
Puddings
Cheese

Vegetarian cheese w/case
Half & half
Cottage cheese
Ricotta cheese
Caseinates

Curd
Dairy solids
Cultured dairy

**Caseins**: a protein found in milk
Ref. #15

**Galactose:** is a greek word - Gala = milk and Ose = sugar
Ref. #16

**Whey in all forms**

**Whey protein, Concentrate**

**Hydrolysates:** which include casein, milk protein and whey

**Lactose:** a sugar found in milk & dairy products

**Lactoglobulin:** a whey protein of cows and other mammals.
Ref. #17

**Lactulose:** is made from lactose (the sugar found in milk), and contains two simple sugars – galactose and glucose
Ref. #18

**Recaldent**: is an ingredient derived from casein, part of the protein found in cow's milk. You can find recaldent in MI paste which is used for teeth.
Ref. #19

## HERE ARE SOME OTHER FOODS THAT LADAIRYA MOO MAY BE HIDING IN:

Baked goods
Chocolate
Processed meats
Non-dairy products
Non-dairy fat solids

Natural flavorings
Lactic acid
Caramel
Flavorings
Artificial butter

Salad dressings
Bread crumbs
Soups
Protein shakes
Medications

Gravies
Dips
Crackers
Nougats

**A Peanut Allergy is serious and can be life-threatening.** The allergic reaction is an adverse immune response to the protein in peanuts. Reactions vary from person to person and can range from lasting a few minutes to a few hours  Ref. #20

Beware when eating out, especially when eating at Asian or Mexican restaurants, as many use sauces and marinades that could include peanuts or peanut oil. Another place to be extra careful is at ice cream shops because peanuts are used as ingredients and toppings. Ref. #21

Peanuts are referred to by many names such as: ground nuts, goobers, or goober peas and are part of the legume family which include beans, peas, chickpeas, lentils and soy beans. This allergy is not the same as a tree nut allergy.

Always check labels to look for phrases that say: May contain, or manufactured in a facility that also processes peanuts.

## BEWARE

### PEANUT THE KID IS IN THESE:

Beer nuts
Arachis
Ground nuts
Flavored nuts
Peanut butter
Peanut paste
Peanut syrup
Peanut  butter morsels
Cold pressed peanut oil
Expelled peanut oil
Extruded peanut oil
Satay: a peanut sauce
Fenugreek: used in curry dishes

Goobers
Artificial nuts
Mixed nuts
Peanuts
Peanut flour
Peanut sauce

### ? CAN AN ALLERGIC REACTION OCCUR BY SMELLING A PEANUT? ?

Smelling a peanut won't cause an allergic reaction, but a reaction can be triggered by inhaling airborne peanut particles. Those particles are released when peanuts are chopped, mixed, chewed, and so on. If there's enough peanut protein in the air, including on the breath of another person, it can be enough to cause a life-threatening allergic reaction. Carrying an Epi-pen can help children stay safe. Ref. #22

**BEWARE**
**Peanut the Kid** Could be hiding in these foods

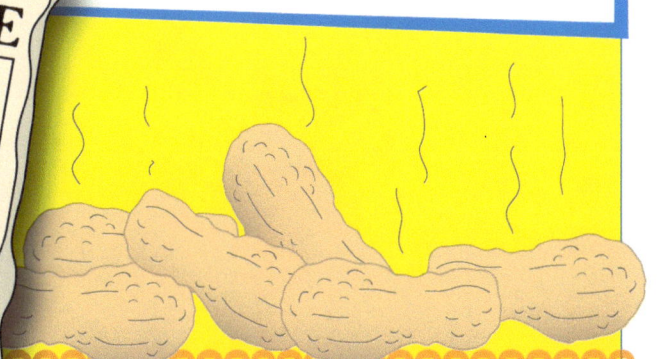

## PEANUT THE KID SOMETIMES SNEAKS HIS WAY INTO THESE FOODS:

| | | | | |
|---|---|---|---|---|
| Baking mixes | **Baked Goods:** Cookies, cakes, muffins, pies, bars, brownies, etc. | | | Candy |
| Chocolate | Cereals | Energy bars/Protein bars | Asian food | Egg rolls |
| Mexican food | Fried foods | Artificial flavorings | Natural flavorings | |
| Nougat | Trail mixes | Granola | Pastries | Pesto |
| Salad dressings | Praline | | | |

Hydrolyzed plant protein     Hydrolyzed vegetable protein     Lupine: is a legume
Peanut marzipan or mazapan: comes from Latin America     Mandelonas: fake nut
Mole sauce: a thick chocolate-based sauce used in Mexican cooking.
**Chili:** peanut butter is sometimes used as a  thickening agent or flavor enhancer.
Be sure to ask  when ordering this in restaurants

# SHELLFISH ALLERGY

**A Shellfish Allergy can be life-threatening.** The allergic reaction comes in the form of an adverse immune response (hives, difficulty breathing, vomiting...). An allergic reaction is triggered by eating shellfish, but can also be caused by smelling the shellfish in the air as it's being cooked. Note that a shellfish reaction can become severe very quickly.

**Shellfish intolerance/sensitivity** are conditions that aren't usually life-threatening. A typical result would be a person having a hard time digesting shellfish in the form of symptoms such as bloating, stomach pains, and/or diarrhea.
Ref. #23

If you have a fish allergy, it doesn't mean you will also have a shellfish allergy. Always consult your doctor/allergist before consuming it.

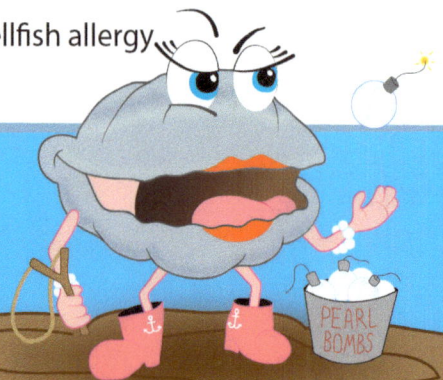

CALAMITY:
CAUSING TROUBLE
EVERYWHERE SHE GOES

**CRUSTACEANS:**

| Crawfish | Crayfish | Ecrevisse |
|---|---|---|
| Lobster | Langouste | Langoustine |
| Coral | Tamalley | Shrimp |
| Prawns | Crevettes | Krill |
| Barnacle | | |

**MOLLUSKS**

| Clams | Mussels |
|---|---|
| Oysters | Scallops |
| Cockles | Octopus |
| Abalone | Conch |
| Limpets | Whelks |
| Periwinkles | Sea Urchin |
| Cuttlefish | Sea cucumber |

Snail: also known as gastropods, escargot
Squid: calamari
Ref. #24

CALAMITY IS ALSO KNOWN AS MOLLY MOLLUSK

## CALAMITY MAY ALSO BE HIDING OUT IN SOME OF THE ITEMS BELOW:

| Crabcakes | Fish sticks | Fish nuggets | Jambalaya | Sushi |
|---|---|---|---|---|
| Gumbo | Salad dressing | Sauces | Fish stock | Asian food |
| Ceviche | Cioppino | Callaloo | Curanto | Fruits de mer |
| Paella | Sashimi | Shrimp cocktail | Lobster bisque | She-crab soup |
| Sliced fish soup | Shrimp Saganaki | Pizza toppings | Clam chowders/soups | |

**Glucosamine is used in some supplements and is made from the shells of shellfish**

| Bouillabaisse | Cuttlefish ink | Soy sauce | Seafood flavoring | Surimi |
|---|---|---|---|---|

Ref. #25

**A Soy Allergy can be, but is rarely, life-threatening.** A severe allergic reaction comes in the form of an anaphylactic shock. Lesser, but still definite signs of a soy allergy are hives, swelling (typically lips, face, tongue, and throat), wheezing, diarrhea, and vomiting. This allergy is triggered by ingesting soy.
Ref. #26

**Children should avoid soy in all forms.**
Soy is part of the bean and legume family. Children who are allergic to soy might or might not be allergic to other beans. Consult with your doctor/allergist determine this.
Soy is found in many products as an oil, protein source, thickener and more. Soybean oil and Soy Lecithin are found in many convenience foods on supermarket shelves. Remember to always read your labels. In the U.S., the word "SOY" must be included on food labels where potential allergens are listed if it's an ingredient, or if there's any chance of cross-contamination from the factory where the food was manufactured.
Ref. #27

## SID SOY LOOKS FRIENDLY BUT BEWARE HE'S IN ALMOST EVERYTHING YOU EAT

| | |
|---|---|
| Soy | Soy lecithin |
| Soy albumin | Soy cheese |
| Soy fiber | Soy flour |
| Soy ice cream | Soy milk |
| Soy nuts | Soy sprouts |
| Soy yogurt | |

| | |
|---|---|
| Soybean | Soybean curd |
| Soybean granules | Edamame |
| Miso | Natto |
| Tofu | Seitan |

**Soy protein:** concentrate, hydrolyzed, isolate
**Sauces:** soy, shoyu, tamari, teriyaki, Worcestershire

## HERE ARE SOME OTHER FOODS THAT SID SOY MAY BE HIDING IN:

| | | | |
|---|---|---|---|
| Infant formula | Protein shakes | Taco seasoning | Nutrition supplements |
| Imitation bacon bits | Vegetarian burgers | Gravies | Tempeh    Crackers |
| Vegetarian dishes | Puddings | Candy | Processed meats and cheeses |
| Cocoa/Cocoa powder | Hot chocolate | Pretzels | Chocolate/Chocolate chips |
| Carob | Ketchup | Potato chips | Veggie starch |
| Thickening agents | Natural flavorings | Guar gum | Health bars |
| Granola bars | Vegetable oils | Margarine | Cooking sprays |
| Dressings | Marinades | Seasonings | Mayonnaise |
| Bouillon cubes | Peanut butter | Canned tuna | Mono and Diglycerides |

**Monosodium glutamate:** a flavor enhancer also known as MSG
**Breads:** sliced breads, rolls, hamburger buns, hot dog buns
**Baked goods:** cakes, cookies, muffins, pies, donuts

# TREE NUT ALLERGY

**Tree Nut Allergies are serious and can be life-threatening.** This allergy triggers an adverse immune response (much the same as the other Infamous 8 allergies) to the protein in tree nuts. Having a peanut allergy is not the same as being allergic to tree nuts and usually lasts a lifetime with less than 10 percent of sufferers growing out of it.    Ref. #28

People who are allergic to a specific tree nut may be able to tolerate other nuts, but this is something you should discuss with your doctor/allergist.

The FDA requires by state law that the top eight food allergens must be listed on the label of a product. However, products manufactured overseas may not include allergen information on their labels. Many tree nuts are used for oil, flavor, texture, and more. On American products, look for the words "May contain or be processed in a facility with tree nuts."    Ref. #29

| | |
|---|---|
| Walnut | White walnut |
| Black walnut | Pistachio |
| Butternut | Beechnut |
| Brazil nut | Bush nut |
| Chestnut | Ginko nut |
| Hickory nut | Lichee nut |
| Macadamia nut | Hazelnut |
| Nangai nut | Pine nut |
| Shea nut | *Coconut |

Ref. #30

## LET'S TALK ABOUT COCONUTS:

*The Food and Drug Administration lists coconut as a tree nut, but it's actually a drupe, and falls into the same category as stone fruits like nectarines, peaches, plums, and cherries. Most people who are allergic to tree nuts can safely eat coconut, but this is something you should always discuss with your doctor/allergist.

Ref. #31

**Nutmeg isn't a nut.** It's a spice derived from a seed, so people with a tree nut allergy should be free to enjoy it. As always, discuss this with your doctor/allergist first.

**Be aware when dining out.** Always speak to your server about your food allergy, and ask them to explain the ingredients in dishes you're interested in. It's also important to discuss their food handling policies to ensure you're in a restaurant that's safe to eat at. Better safe than sorry!

## LOOK OUT!

### THE TREE NUT BANDIT CAN BE HANGING AROUND IN THESE, SO ALWAYS BE CAREFUL.

| | | |
|---|---|---|
| Nutella | Baked goods | Pecan pie |
| Cookies | Cakes | Pastries |
| Muffins | Breads | Cereals |
| Crackers | Marzipan | Nougat |
| Praline | Nut milks | Nut pastes |

Nut butters: almond, hazelnut, walnut, and pistachio

Nut oils: walnut oil, pistachio oil,  pecan oil, almond oil, and hazelnut oil

Nut extracts: almond, walnut, pecan, hazelnut, and pistachio

Nut flours/Meals: almond, walnuts, pecans, and hazelnuts

### THE TREE NUT BANDIT IS NUTZ. HE CAN BE HANGING AROUND HERE TOO.

| | | |
|---|---|---|
| Toys | Medications | Cosmetics |
| Cold cuts | Candy | Chocolate |
| Granola | Trail mixes | Pesto |

Frozen desserts
Flavored coffees
Natural flavorings/Artificial flavorings
Mortadella: pistachios lurking in here
Energy bars/Protein bars
Ethnic buisine - Asian, Indian
Sauces/Soups/Marinades
Salad dressings
Pre-packaged foods
Vegetarian meals

# WHEAT ALLERGY

**A Wheat Allergy can be life-threatening**, and triggers an immune response to the protein in wheat. A person with a wheat allergy can experience various symptoms ranging from mild skin reactions such as hives, all the way up to a severe, life-threatening reaction in a matter of minutes. Wheat allergy is very common in children, but approximately about 65 percent outgrow a wheat allergy by the time they reach their teens.
Ref. #32

Be aware of foods that don't contain wheat but could be cross-contaminated as a result of the manufacturing process. Check labels for ingredients and manufacturing details. Alternately, there are many non-wheat flour alternatives such as oat, amaranth, corn, sorghum, soy, tapioca or potato starch, and quinoa.

Those with wheat allergies can typically still eat gluten, but since it's in so many convenience foods—usually described as starch or modified food starch—it might be best to go gluten-free and use only certified products. Wheat: a grain used as an ingredient in cereals, pastas, and breads. A wheat allergy is different than a gluten intolerance or celiac disease.

## LET'S TALK ABOUT GLUTEN

**Gluten** is a protein found in wheat, barley, and rye. It is mainly found in food, but it can even be found in cosmetics and toiletries.

**Gluten intolerance/sensitivity** are the same thing, and result in digestive problems that might include bloating, stomach pain, nausea, and diarrhea. This isn't the same as celiac disease.

**Celiac disease** is an autoimmune disorder in which the body's reaction to the protein, gluten is an attack on the small intestine. Celiac disease damages the villi that line inner parts of the small intestine, making it very difficult for the body to absorb nutrients into the bloodstream. In addition to gastric upset, unmanaged celiac disease can also result in the development of other autoimmune disorders such as anemia, osteoporosis, and even intestinal cancers.
Ref. #33

## BEWARE THE WHEAT-GI IS IN HERE:

**Wheat:** also known as germ, gluten, grass, malt, sprouts, bran, durum starch
**Bulgur:** cracked wheat grains
**Club wheat:** used for making pastry flour
**Durum:** a wheat with slightly higher gluten & protein content
**Einkorn:** a wild species of wheat
**Emmer:** a wheat also known as farro
**Farina:** a form of milled wheat used for cereal
**Kamut:** also called Khorasan wheat or Pharaoh grain
**Wheat bran hydrolysate**   **Wheat protein isolate**
**Wheat berries**
**Matzoh:** a flat piece of unleavened bread used for passover
**Seitan:** used as a meat substitute in vegetarian dishes.
**Hydrolyzed wheat protein:** (HVP) a flavor enhancer that may also contain small amounts of MSG
**Vital wheat gluten:** beware, this is added to many breads

| Bread crumbs | Cereal extract | Couscous |
| Cracker meal | Wheat germ oil | Triticale |
| Semolina | Sprouted wheat | Spelt |
| Wheat grass | Pasta | |
| Whole wheat: all forms | | |

**Flours include:**

| All purpose | Bread | Cake |
| Durum | Enriched | Graham |
| High gluten | High protein | Pastry |
| Self-rising | | |

## WHEAT GI MOVES INTO THINGS QUICKLY SO LOOK OUT. HE CAN BE HIDING IN HERE

| Bake mixes | Baked goods | Cereals | Breaded or fried foods | Dressings |
| Marinades | Gravies | Soy sauce | Processed meats | Soups |
| Sauces | Frozen desserts | Surimi | Natural & artificial flavorings | Pretzels |
| Coffee substitutes | Play-Doh | Colorings | Glucose syrup | Vegetable gums |
| Medications | Root beer | Hot dogs | Packaged puddings | Cereal beverages |

Potato chips/ fries: may contain wheat starch     Candy/chocolate/ Malted chocolate
Instant chocolate drink mixes     MSG - monosodium glutamate
Cottage cheese - with modified starch or other wheat-containing ingredients
Make-up     **Hair products:** Shampoos, conditioners     **Skin care:** Lotions/creams     Dog food

# WHEN CONCERNED WITH FOOD ALLERGIES, ALWAYS READ THE LABELS.

**Allergen labeling for packaged foods sold in the U.S. is dictated by an act of Congress known as FALCPA** (Food Allergen Labeling and Consumer Protection Act) *(FALCPA regulations apply only to foods regulated by the FDA, which DO NOT include meat, poultry, and eggs.)* Ref.# 34

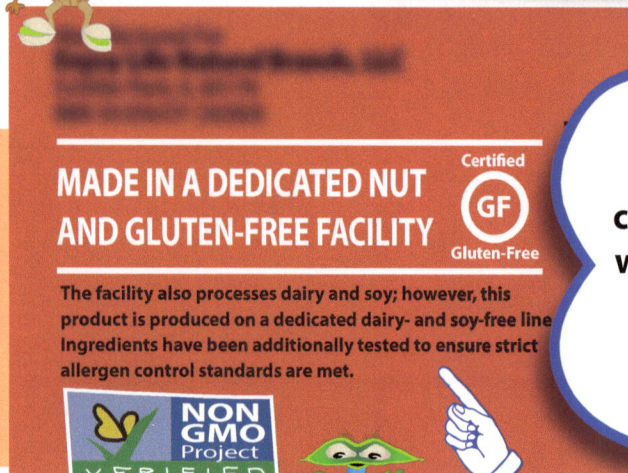

**MADE IN A DEDICATED NUT AND GLUTEN-FREE FACILITY**

Certified **GF** Gluten-Free

The facility also processes dairy and soy; however, this product is produced on a dedicated dairy- and soy-free line Ingredients have been additionally tested to ensure strict allergen control standards are met.

NON GMO Project VERIFIED

**Reading labels on food products is confusing enough without having to deal with allergen issues. Is it really safe?**

Calories per gram:
Fat 9 • Carbohydrates 4 • Protein 4

**Ingredients:** Stone Ground White Corn, Sunflower Oil or Corn Oil, Sea Salt, Water, Trace of Lime.

Our vendors follow Good Manufacturing Practices to segregate ingredients to avoid cross contact with allergens. Made on shared equipment with milk, tree nuts & soy.

**Whole Fiber 100% Whole Wheat Bread**

NO Bromate
NO Hydrogenated Oil
0 grams *Trans* Fat
NO Saturated Fats

INGREDIENTS: WATER, 100% WHOLE GRAIN WHOLE WHEAT FLOUR, SOY FIBER, WHEAT GLUTEN, SUGAR CONTAINS 2% OR LESS OF THE FOLLOWING: YEAST, MOLASSES, SALT, CALCIUM SULFATE, PRESERVATIVES (CALCIUM PROPIONATE, PROPIONIC ACID, PHOSPHORIC ACID), GUAR GUM, ETHOXYLATED MONO AND DIGLYCERIDES, SOYBEAN OIL (NON-HYDROGENATED), MONO AND DIGLYCERIDES, FUMARIC ACID, SODIUM STEAROYL LACTYLATE, AMMONIUM SULFATE, MONOCALCIUM PHOSPHATE, ASCORBIC ACID ADDED AS A DOUGH CONDITIONER, AZODICARBONAMIDE, ENZYMES, CALCIUM PEROXIDE, FOLIC ACID, VITAMIN D3.
**CONTAINS: WHEAT, SOYBEAN.** A75371

**Allergy Advisory:** Produced on the same bakery equipment as baked goods containing eggs, nuts or seeds. Therefore, this product may inadvertently contain eggs, nuts or seeds to which some people may be allergic.

**Every label is different per manufacturer. What and where cross-contact allergen information is listed is optional.**

Sugars 9g
**Protein** 5g

| Vitamin A | 0% | • | Vitamin C | 2% |
|---|---|---|---|---|
| Calcium | 4% | • | Iron | 8% |

* Percent Daily Values are based on a 2,000 calorie diet. Your daily values may be higher or lower depending on your calorie needs.

Contains milk and soy products. Manufactured in a plant that handles peanuts, tree nuts and wheat.

**Nutrition Facts**
Serving Size 1 Bar (60g)
**Calories** 280
Calories from Fat

*Percent Daily Values () are based on a 2,000 diet.

| Amount/Serving | %DV* | Amount/Serving | %DV* |
|---|---|---|---|
| **Total Fat** 14g | **22%** | **Total Carb.** 30g | **10%** |
| Sat. Fat 3g | **14%** | Dietary Fiber 6g | **24%** |
| Trans Fat 0g | | Sugars 14g | |
| **Cholesterol** 5mg | **2%** | **Protein** 10g | **20%** |
| **Sodium** 25mg | **1%** | | |

Vitamin A 2% • Vitamin C 15% • Calcium 15% • Iron 10%

**INGREDIENTS:** Sunflower Seeds, Bananas, Prunes, Cricket Flour (Acheta domesticus), Chicory Root Fiber, Banana Chips (Bananas, Coconut Oil, Honey, Natural Banana Flavor), Flaxseeds, Vanilla Extract, Spices, Sea Salt, Natural Banana Flavor. **CONTAINS COCONUT. IF YOU HAVE A CRUSTACEAN SHELLFISH ALLERGY, YOU MAY BE ALLERGIC TO CRICKETS. MAY CONTAIN TRACES OF PEANUTS, TREE NUTS, WHEAT, MILK, SOY, AND EGG.** MFG. FOR EXO, INC. I BROOKLYN, NY 11231

**READ LABELS CAREFULLY:**
In some products, the cross-contact warning is nowhere near the ingredients list.

**\***

*The information here is only a guideline, a starting point to understanding food labeling. If you have concerns, contact the manufacturer. As always, if you have allergy questions, contact your allergist or physician.*

Knowing how to interpret a food label when grocery shopping will help keep your family safe.

| STOP | The label **CAN** warn you that the product is not safe. |
| --- | --- |

| ? | The label alone **CAN'T** tell you that the product is safe. |
| --- | --- |

Manufacturers **MUST** clearly indicate when any of *The Infamous 8* allergens are *ingredients* in the product: peanuts, tree nuts, eggs, milk, wheat, soybeans, fish, and shellfish.

Manufacturers are **NOT** required to tell you when there is a possibility of cross-contamination with these allergens!

## Same Label - Different Versions

When the ingredient is a derivative of the allergen —for example, "albumin (egg)," the main allergen is listed in the ingredients in parentheses.

Often, the allergen is within the ingredients but not in **bold** and can be hard to find.

Allergens can also be listed both in the ingredients AND have a separate "contains" or "may contain" statement.

Wheat, Milk, and Soy are not listed in ingredients. Eggs are listed in both **Ingredients** and **Contains** sections.

## Nutrition Facts

Serving Size  1/2 oz (14g)

**Amount Per Serving**

| Calories  35 | Calories from Fat 0 |
| --- | --- |

| | % **Daily Value***|
| --- | --- |
| **Total Fat** 0g | 0% |
| Saturated Fat 0g | 0% |
| *Trans* Fat 0g | |
| **Cholesterol**  0mg | 0% |
| | 0% |
| | 3% |
| | 0% |

Vitamin C 2%

Calcium 0        •    Iron

* Percent Daily Values are based 2,000 calo

**Ingredients:** Enriched flour (flour, malted barley, niac educed iron, thiamin mononitra ribo avin, folic ugar, partially h ated cot nseed oil, ructose corn sy ey, eggs, vanilla, na d artificial , salt, leavening (sodiu pyropho nate, monocalcium pho e), lecithin, mono and diglycerides.

**Contains:** Wheat, Milk, Egg, and Soy.

**Ingredients:** Enriched flour (wheat flou ley in, reduced iron, thiamin m bofl n, folic acid), sugar, partially og otter eed oil, high fructose corn sy wh milk) eggs, vanilla, natural and arti ial flav salt, leavening (sodium acid pyrophosphate monocalcium phosphate), lethicin (soy) m glycerides.

This section could also contain additional warnings like "May contain…" and "Manufactured on equipment with…" and are completely voluntary. There are no standards for when they should be used, how they are worded, and where they should be placed.

**THEIR ABSENCE DOES NOT MEAN THE PRODUCT IS SAFE!**

# FOOD ALLERGY AWARENESS

## Common locations where Jake and Ava could experience an allergic reaction.

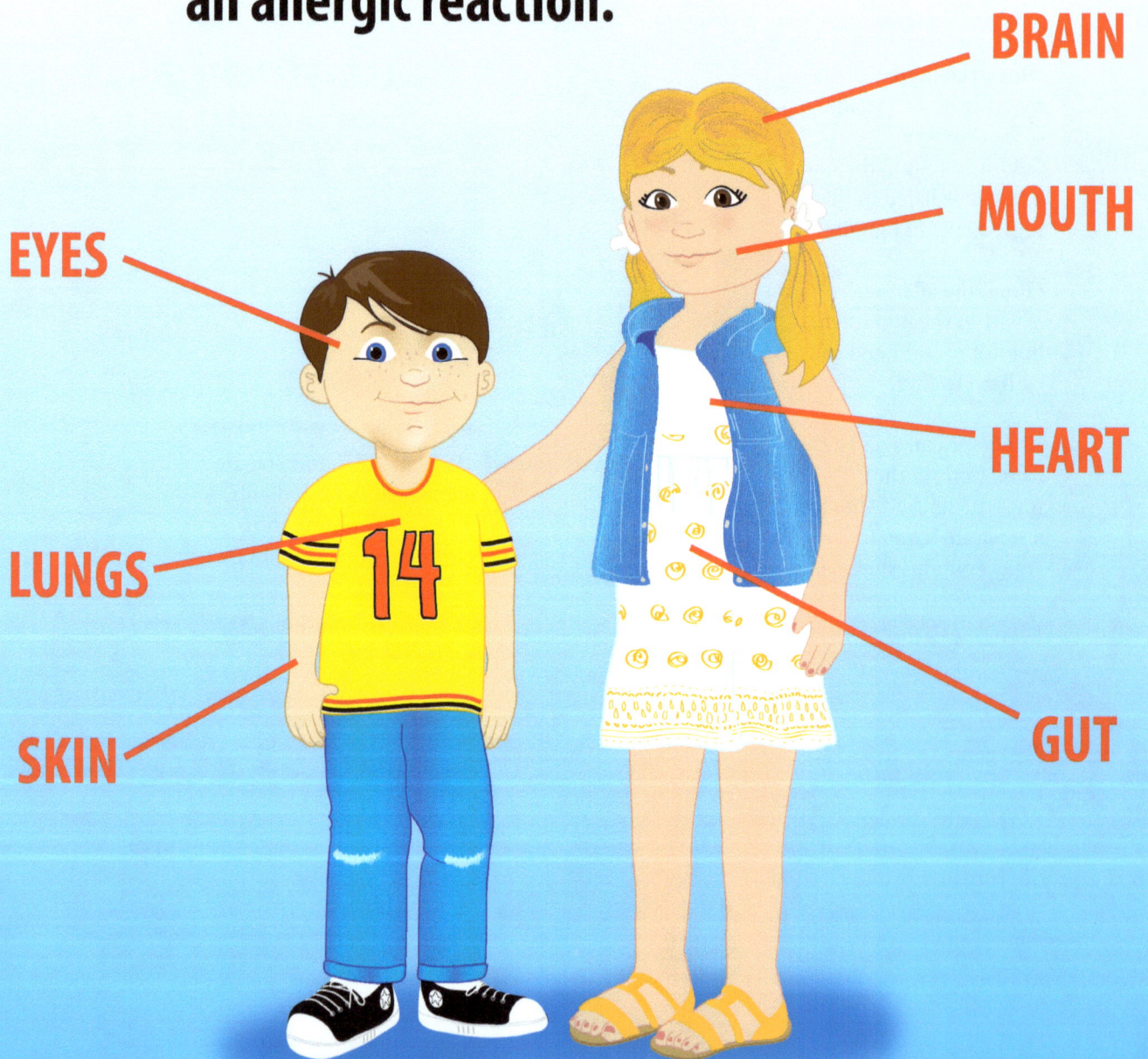

BRAIN

MOUTH

EYES

HEART

LUNGS

SKIN

GUT

14

**Caution:**
Always be aware! Everyone is different, so people can experience additional symptoms/ reactions in parts of the body not listed above.

# Birthday Party Adventure

~

It's an exciting day for Ava and Jake. They're going to a birthday party!
All their classmates will be there.
But the Infamous 8 might be there too, and they could
spoil the party if Ava and Jake aren't careful.

The Infamous 8 are the most common food allergies many children have.
Ava and Jake both have food allergies.

Follow Ava and Jake on their mission as they try to avoid the
Infamous 8 and find the foods that are perfect for them,
so they can have a safe and fun time at the party.

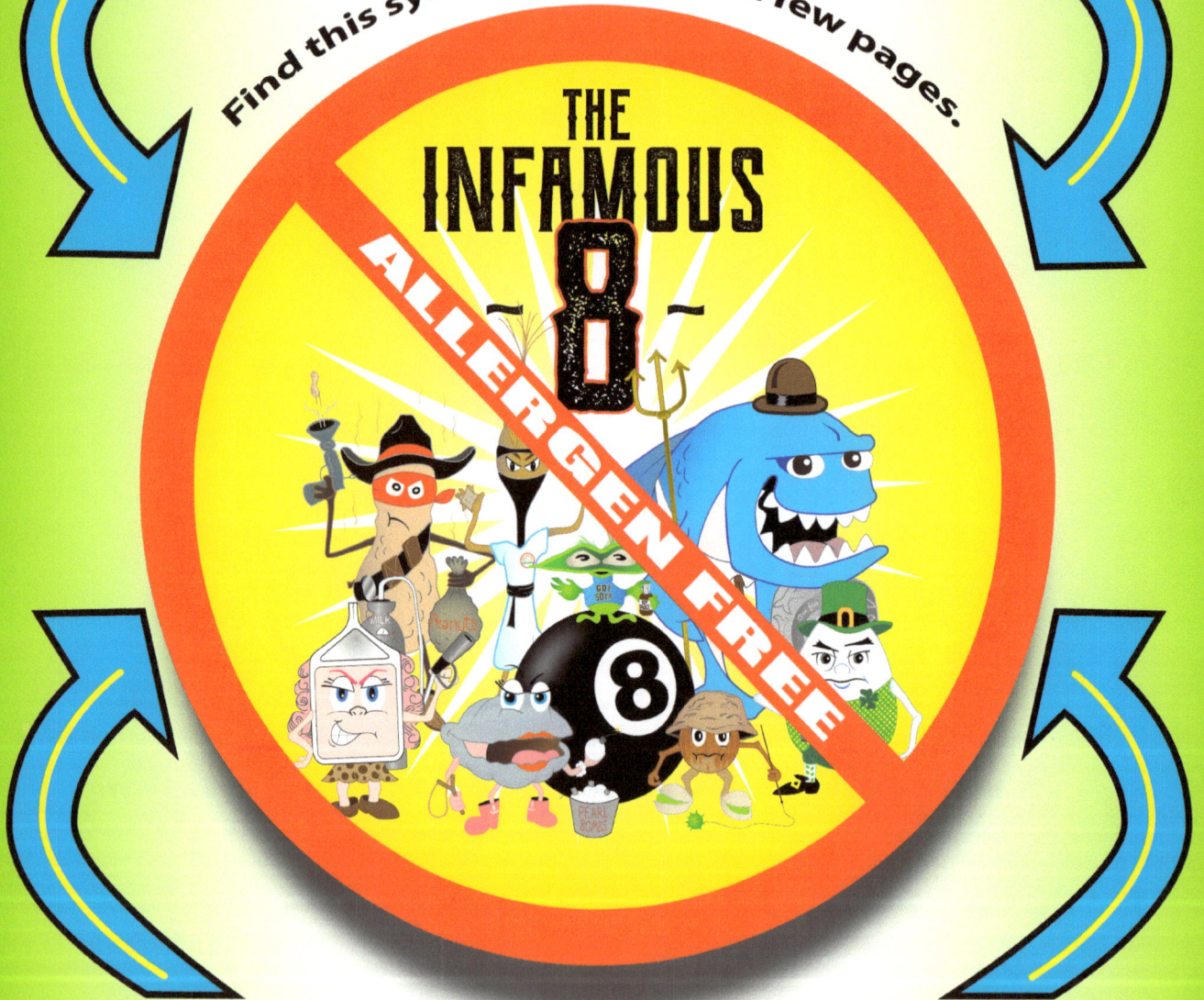

# LOOK!

Find this symbol on the next few pages.

THE INFAMOUS 8

ALLERGEN FREE

This symbol indicates foods that are safe from all of **The Infamous 8** allergens.
In the following story, you can use it to help Ava and Jake find foods they can both eat safely.

Ava and Jake are really excited.

They have been invited to their best friend,

Matthew's, birthday party.

They raid their piggy banks for money to buy him a present.

Their mom drives them to the mall to go shopping.

At the store, they find the perfect present.

They ask the shopkeeper if she can wrap the gift.

Ava carries the gift back to the car proudly.

As Jake walks back to the car, he says,

"Now we're all ready for the party."

"Not so fast Jake," his mother warns.

"You're forgetting something."

Mom says, "I know it's not always fun to have to watch everything you eat to avoid 'The Infamous 8,' but I promise there will be lots of tasty things to enjoy. Just think about where your villians might be hiding, and you'll have a great time."

"Yes, Mom, we'll remember," they both promise.

"I'll also call Matthew's mom to remind her about food allergies."

"Oh please, Mom, don't make a fuss," Ava begs, "It's bad enough being different from the other kids without everyone knowing."

24

The next day, Ava packs her pink allergy bag. In goes Beni–dryl and Epi–man.

Jake packs his blue backpack. In goes Epi—man and Beni—dryl.

ALLERGEN
FREE PIZZA

ALLERGEN
FREE
BROWNIES

Ava's
allergy
bag

Ava takes the delicious food Mom has made for
everyone to share at the party. She can smell the
special villian—free pizza and chocolate brownies
and she and Jake can't wait to eat them.
Jake picks up the present and heads for the car.

Once they get to the party, they see the beautiful birthday buffet.

Ava and Jake's villains are everywhere.

Help Ava and Jake make good food choices by remembering their villains.

EXPLORE! WHO ARE YOUR VILLAINS?
Learn more. Go to pages 2–5 & 8–15 and check the villain files and charts.

What foods should Jake avoid? What things can he enjoy?

These are Jake's villains.

Sid Soy    Peanut the Kid    Wheat Gi    Treenut Bandit

What foods should Ava avoid? What things can she eat?

These are Ava's villains.

Calamity    Brutus    Shamus McScrambler    LaDairya Moo

"Don't forget, we need to watch what we drink too," Ava reminds her brother.

These are Ava's villains.

What drinks can Ava have?

These are Jake's villains.

What drinks can Jake have?

Help Jake and Ava choose a drink that is safe for them at Matthew's party.

Allergy villains can be lurking everywhere. Always read the labels to be sure.

ARE YOUR VILLAINS HIDING HERE? Explore pages 2–5 & 8–15 and check the villain files and charts.

ORGANIC STRAWBERRIES

ORGANIC CHERRIES

CHEESE RICE PUFFS — Contains Milk

TORTILLA CHIPS ALLERGEN FREE

GUACAMOLE ALLERGEN FREE

SALSA ALLERGEN FREE

FRUIT BOWL

WHEAT GRAHAM CRACKERS — contains wheat

ORGANIC RAIS...

ORGANIC NATURAL CALIFORNIA RAISINS

MARSHMALLOWS — contains Soy

Almond YOGURT — non-dairy & lactose free — made with almond milk

ORGANIC SOY YOGURT — Dairy free — made with soy milk

non-dairy CULTURED COCONUT YOGURT — UNSWEETENED — made with coconut milk

Milk Yogurt — made with milk

Milk Yogurt — made with milk

Milk Yogurt — made with milk

BUTTERED POPCORN — CONTAINS MILK

BUTTERED POP CORN — contains milk

YOGURT

VEGETABLE TRAY

WATERMELON

Sour Cream & Onion — contains milk

Nacho seasoned KALE CHIPS — peanut with cashew butter — Gluten Free — Air-Crisped under low heat Never Fried — contains tree nuts

Gluten-free Wheat-free PRETZELS — contains soy

POTATO CHIPS — Cooked in Peanut Oil

organic

organic

organic

organic

Apple Sauce — GLUTEN-FREE NO SUGAR ADDED

CINNAMON Apple Sauce — GLUTEN-FREE NO SUGAR ADDED

HUMMUS DIP — contains tree nuts

CHEESE — contains milk

CRACKERS & CHEESE

Assorted Wheat CRACKERS — contains wheat

"The snacks look great, but we need to watch out there too," says Jake.

Which snacks can Ava have?
Watch out for Ava's villains.

Calamity

Brutus

Shamus McScrambler

LaDairya Moo

Which snacks can Jake enjoy?
Watch out for Jake's villains.

Sid Soy

Peanut the Kid

Wheat Gi

Treenut Bandit

Help Jake and Ava pick a safe snack. Remember, dangerous ingredients can be hiding in your snacks, so be careful when you choose.

WHAT IS SAFE FOR YOU TO EAT? Explore pages 2–5 & 8–15 and check the villain files and charts. (31)

Out on the patio, Matthew's dad is cooking.

There are villains lurking everywhere. Ava and Jake

will have to be careful when choosing what to eat.

On the table labels:
- ORGANIC GRILLED CHICKEN
- ORGANIC CORN
- ORGANIC BEEF HAMBURGER
- HOT DOGS MAY CONTAIN WHEAT & SOY
- GRILLED SHRIMP
- GRILLED SALMON
- CHEDDAR CHEESE contains milk
- Gluten-free Wheat-free HOT DOG BUNS Free from Top 8 Allergens
- Gluten-free Wheat-free HAMBURGER BUNS Free from Top 8 Allergens
- BBQ SAUCE CONTAINS SOY
- Mayonnaise contains eggs
- THE INFAMOUS 8 ALLERGEN FREE ORGANIC KETCHUP Made with Goodness
- MUSTARD 100% Natural may contain wheat

**W**hat things should Jake avoid? What things can he eat?

Watch out for Jake's villains.

What things should Ava avoid?  What things can she enjoy?

Watch out for Ava's villains.

Sid Soy    Peanut the Kid    Wheat Gi    Treenut Bandit

Calamity    Brutus    Shamus McScrambler    LaDairya Moo

WHERE ARE YOUR VILLIANS HIDING? Explore pages 2–5 & 8–15 and check the villain files and charts.

**S**oon, it's time to sing "Happy Birthday" to Matthew and let him blow out the candles on his cake.

The cake is made with wheat flour, eggs, and buttercream frosting.

Can Ava or Jake have cake? If they can't have cake, what can they safely eat for dessert?

Explore pages 28 & 29 and help Ava and Jake find villian–free choices they can eat.

Next, it's time to open the presents.

Matthew loves all his gifts, especially the one from Ava and Jake.

The children play with all the new toys

until it is time for their parents to pick them up.

"Did you have a fun time?" Mom asks as they buckle their seatbelts.

"Awesome," Jake says. "Avoiding allergy villains is easier than I thought. There was lots of safe stuff to eat."

"The brownies you made were great, Mom," says Ava. "Can you teach me how to make the recipe?"

"Sure, honey, as soon as we get home."

PARTY TIME

PARTY TIME

When they get home, they go upstairs to change clothes.

Ava puts her pink allergy bag back on top of her dresser.

Jake puts his blue backpack on his chair.

HOME

37

JAKE'S ALLERGY BAG

Epi-man and Beni-dryl didn't have to come to the rescue today, but it's always smart for Ava and Jake to bring them everywhere, just in case.

# SWAPPING

Knowing what you are allergic to is the first step.
Learning more about smart substitutions can also help keep you safe.
Here are some smart substitutions to try.

Also included are common allergy acronyms to look for
on labels, restaurant menus, and elsewhere.

# SUBSTITUTION LIST FOR MILK/DAIRY

**MILK SUBSTITUTES:** rice milk, coconut milk, almond milk oat milk, soy milk, hemp milk, cashew milk, and hazelnut milk. Some brands are **Califia, New Barn, So Delicious, Silk, Rice Dream, Ripple pea milk, and Forager.**

**CREAM SUBSTITUTES:** coconut creamer, coconut whipped cream, rice whip cream, rice creamer, soy sour cream, soy whipping cream, or soy creamer. Some brands are **So Delicious, Rice Dream, Califia, and Coconut Cloud.**

**DAIRY-FREE CHEESE SUBSTITUTES:** soy cheese, rice cheese, nut-based cheese alternatives. My favorite brand is **Daiya** because their cheese melts easily. They make many different kinds of cheeses including mozzarella, provolone, gruyere, and cheddar.

**YOGURT SUBSTITUTES:** coconut, almond, cashew, soy. Some of the brands I like are **So Delicious, Kate Hill, and Forager.**

**BUTTER/OIL SUBSTITUTES:** dairy-free, non-hydrogenated margarine, organic coconut spread, organic virgin coconut oil, organic extra virgin olive oil, and organic cold-pressed canola oil for cooking, baking, or spreading. Some of the ones I like are **Earth Balance** and **Spectrum.**

✳ **If you have the time, making your own milk is the best, and it's easy to do.**
**(Also, be sure to purchase unsweetened non-dairy milk if you're baking with it.)**

## RECIPE — Sweetened Condensed Non-Dairy Milk

### Ingredients

2 cups
Dairy-free milk

1/2 cup
Organic cane sugar

4 Tbsp Dairy-free butter

1 tsp Vanilla extract

### Directions

1. Combine all of the ingredients in a medium-size pan, and heat on medium-low for about 50 minutes, stirring occasionally.
2. The Milk will become slightly thick in consistency
3. When it's done, you should have about 1 cup. Place in refrigerator up to 3 days.
You can use this for a recipe that calls for condensed milk.

LA DAIRYA MOO
WON'T BE HERE

✳ If you don't have the time to make your own milk, **Nature's Charm's** sweetened condensed coconut milk is a great brand to buy.

## RECIPE — Buttermilk Replacement

### Ingredients

1 cup
Milk of choice
(I prefer coconut)

1 Tbsp Organic lemon juice
or Apple cider vinegar

### Directions

Place ingredients in bowl.
Let it sit for 5 to 10 minutes and use.
Equals = 1 cup of buttermilk

## EGG REPLACEMENT CHART

The list below can be used to replace eggs in baking recipes. They all serve as a binding and/or leavening agents. The purpose of a binder is to help hold the recipe together. The purpose of the leavening agent is to help baked goods rise.

\* Please note: Not all of these replacements can be used for doubling recipes.

Keep in mind that the texture of the baked product may also change and become denser or grittier.

**Ener-G Egg Replacer:** follow the instructions on the label

**Bob's Red Mill Egg Replacer:** follow the instructions the label

**Namastee Foods Egg Replacer:** (as a binder) follow the instructions on the label

**Vegan egg:** (also another egg replacer) you can also use this to make scrambled eggs, as well as in baking. Read label for instructions

Unsweetened organic applesauce: ½ cup = 1 egg replacer

Organic mashed banana: ½ cup = 1 egg replacer

Organic pumpkin puree: ½ cup = 1 egg replacer

Silken tofu: 1/4 cup of whipped silken tofu = 1 egg replacer

Vinegar and baking soda: 1 tsp of baking soda mixed with 1 Tbsp of apple cider vinegar = 1 egg replacer

---

## RECIPE Flax meal or Ground flax seed

**Ingredients**

1 Tbsp Flax meal

2 Tbsp Warm water

**Directions**

Mix together until it forms a gel-like consistency - about 5 to 10 minutes. This will equal 1 egg

---

## RECIPE Chia seeds - Egg replacer

**Ingredients**

1 Tbsp Chia seeds

3 Tbsp Warm water

**Directions**

Mix together until it forms a gel-like consistency - about 5 to 10 minutes. This will equal 1 egg

---

### SHAMUS McSCRAMBLER WON'T BE HERE

---

Sources

//www.egglesscooking.com/egg-substitutes/

http://www.peta.org/living/food/egg-replacements

# SUBSTITUTION LIST FOR FIN-FISH & SHELLFISH

**NO SEAFOOD HERE:**

| | | |
|---|---|---|
| Beef | Pork | Chicken |
| Turkey | Sausage | Lamb |
| Bison | Veal | |

Protein shakes     Vegetable protein

Omega-3 supplements made with flaxseed or plant-derived oils

http://www.foodfacts.com/fish/

BRUTUS AND CALAMITY
WON'T BE HERE

# SUBSTITUTION LIST FOR SOY

**THERE ARE MANY SOY-FREE OPTIONS. HERE ARE SOME THAT I LIKE:**

SOY MILK: replace with almond, coconut, rice, hemp, oat milk

MAYONNAISE: replace with avocado oil mayo or coconut vegan mayo

YOGURT: brands to try include **So Delicious** coconut yogurt or **Kate Hill** almond yogurt

SOUR CREAM: replace with unsweetened almond/coconut yogurt

CHEESE: **Daiya**, almond or rice cheese

BUTTER/OILS: soy-free organic coconut spread, organic virgin coconut oil, organic extra virgin olive oil for cooking, baking, or spreading. The ones I use are - **Earth Balance** (soy-free) & **Earth Balance** coconut spread

SOY/TERIYAKI SAUCE: replace with coconut aminos

TEMPEH: replace with Hempeh, a great alternative made from hemp seeds

MISO: replace with chickpea or adzuki bean miso. Try the **River Miso** brand

NO WORRIES
SID SOY WON'T BE HERE

# SUBSTITUTION LIST FOR PEANUT & TREE NUT

Seeds are a great alternative to Peanuts and Tree Nuts

| | |
|---|---|
| Pumpkin seeds | Sunflower seeds |
| Chia seeds | Hemp seeds |
| Flax seeds | Seed butters |

My favorite seed butters are pumpkin seed butter and sunflower seed butter. Both contain healthy fats, protein, and are high in Omega-3 fatty acids.

PEANUT THE KID & THE
TREE NUT BANDIT WON'T BE IN HERE

# SUBSTITUTION LIST FOR WHEAT

**WHEAT-FREE SUBSTITUTION FLOURS:**  (All of the flours listed below are also gluten-free.)

| | | |
|---|---|---|
| Oat flour | Sorghum flour | Brown rice |
| Sweet rice flour | Cassava flour | Potato starch |
| Chickpea flour | Quinoa flour | Chia flour |
| Amaranth flour | Banana flour | Coconut flour |
| Almond meal/flour | Xanthan gum | Corn flour |
| Hemp flour | Tapioca starch | Millet flour |
| White rice flour | Buckwheat flour | Arrowroot flour |
| Coffee flour | Corn meal flour | Lupin flour (*made from a legume*) |

## WHEAT AND GLUTEN-FREE FLOUR RECIPE

## THE INFAMOUS 8 FLOUR

# RECIPE  The Infamous 8 Flour

**Ingredients**

2 Cups white rice flour

1 Cup tapioca flour

1 Cup Sorghum flour

1 tsp Xanthum gum

**Directions**

1. Combine all ingredients and store in an air-tight container.

Makes 4 Cups of flour.
*Substitute for Wheat flour

**This flour is used for the recipes provided in this book.**

THE WHEAT-GI WON'T BE LURKING HERE

# COMMON ALLERGY ACRONYMS

**MA** — *Milk Allergy*

CMPI – Cow's Milk Protein Intolerance
CMPA – Cow's Milk Protein Allergy
DF – Dairy Free
LF – Lactose Free
LI – Lactose Intolerant

**WF** — *Wheat Free*

CF – Celiac Friendly
CD – Celiac Disease
GF – Gluten Free

**EA** — *Egg Allergy*

**TNA** — *Tree Nut Allergy*

**SF** — *Soy Free*

**SFA** — *Seafood Allergy* Includes Shellfish Fish

**PA** — *Peanut Allergy*

**DPH** — *Diphenhydramine (Benadryl)*

**EPI** — *Epinephrine Injector (Epi-pen)*

These are only a few of the acronyms to be aware of. They may or may not appear on packaging, labels, and restaurant menus. This should not be used as medical advice. Check with your physician, or allergist for more information.

## OTHER COMMON ACRONYMS

FA – Food Allergy
FF – Free From
LFD – Lactose Free Diet
LTFA – Life Threatening Food Allergy
MFA – Multiple Food Allergies

# Easy
# Allergen-Free
# ~ Recipes ~

The following recipes contain substitutes for common cooking
ingredients found in the kitchen. They aren't perfect for everyone,
so check with a doctor or allergist to be sure.
These are designed for the whole family to participate.
Difficulty levels, from easy to hard, are located
in the top, right-hand corner of the page.
These recipes need to be made as indicated,
if not, texture or consistency may vary.

Easy                    Hard

# ~ NOTES ~

# LIQUID & DRY MEASURE CONVERSION CHARTS

## DRY MEASURE CONVERSIONS

| 1 C | = | 8 fl oz | = | 16 Tbsp | = | 48 tsp | = | 237 mL |
|---|---|---|---|---|---|---|---|---|
| 3/4 C | = | 6 fl oz | = | 12 Tbsp | = | 36 tsp | = | 177 mL |
| 2/3 C | = | 5 1/3 fl oz | = | 10 2/3 Tbsp | = | 32 tsp | = | 158 mL |
| 1/2 C | = | 4 fl oz | = | 8 Tbsp | = | 24 tsp | = | 118 mL |
| 1/3 C | = | 2 2/3 fl oz | = | 5 1/3 Tbsp | = | 16 tsp | = | 79 mL |
| 1/4 C | = | 2 fl oz | = | 4 Tbsp | = | 12 tsp | = | 59 mL |
| 1/8 C | = | 1 fl oz | = | 2 Tbsp | = | 6 tsp | = | 30 mL |
| 1/16 C | = | 1/2 fl oz | = | 1 Tbsp | = | 3 tsp | = | 15 mL |

## LIQUID MEASURE CONVERSIONS

| | | | | | | | |
|---|---|---|---|---|---|---|---|
| 1 gal | 4 qt | 8 pt | 16 C | 128 fl oz | 3.79 L | | |
| 1/2 gal | 2 qt | 4 pt | 8 C | 64 fl oz | 1.89 L | | |
| 1/4 gal | 1 qt | 2 pt | 4 C | 32 fl oz | .95 L | | |
| | 1/2 qt | 1 pt | 2 C | 16 fl oz | .47 L | | |
| | 1/4 qt | 1/2 pt | 1 C | 8 fl oz | .24 L | | |
| | | | 1/2 C | 4 fl oz | .12 L | 8 Tbsp | 24 tsp |
| | | | 1/4 C | 2 fl oz | .06 L | 4 Tbsp | 12 tsp |
| | | | 1/8 C | 1 fl oz | .03 L | 2 Tbsp | 6 tsp |
| | | | | 1/2 fl oz | .015 L | 1 Tbsp | 3 tsp |

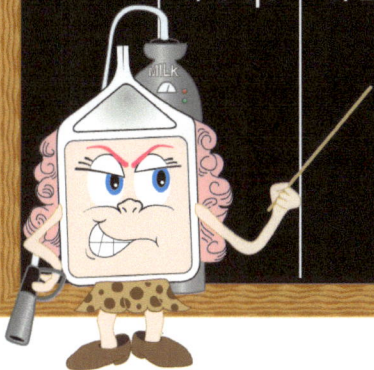

## Chart Terminology

C = cup   Tbsp = Tablespoon   tsp = teaspoon   oz = ounces
mL = milliliters   gal = gallons   qt = quart   pt = pint
L = liters   fl oz = fluid ounces

FLOUR BLEND RECIPE
# THE INFAMOUS 8

# INFAMOUS 8 FLOUR BLEND

**Yields 4 cups**

## Ingredients:

2 C white rice flour

1 C tapioca flour
(also known as tapioca starch)

1 C sorghum flour

1 tsp xanthan gum

## Directions:

**1** Place all ingredients into a 1-gallon storage bag.

**2** Shake until flour is well blended.

**3** Store in a glass mason jar or large storage container until you're ready to use.

Use this mixture in the recipes unless otherwise indicated in this book. You can multiply this recipe as needed if you need to do a lot of baking.

# CHEWY, CRUNCHY OATMEAL COOKIES

Yields about 24 cookies

## Ingredients:

Dry:

1 ½  C organic gluten-free old-fashion rolled oats

1 ½  C Infamous 8 flour blend

1  tsp baking powder

1  tsp organic sea salt

1  tsp cinnamon

¾  C organic raisins

¾  C organic brown sugar

½  C vegan cane sugar

Wet:

Flax-Gel - 2 Tbsp Golden flaxmeal*

4 Tbsp Warm water*

*Combine together in a small bowl, and let rest for 5 to 10 minutes until thickened

½ C organic expeller pressed canola oil or organic unrefined virgin coconut oil, melted. (organic filtered extra virgin olive oil can be substituted)

2 Tbsp unsweetened organic applesauce

## Directions:

1. Preheat the oven to 375F.

2. Line two cookie sheets with parchment paper. Set aside.

3. Prepare flax-gel and set aside until ready to use.

4. In a 1-gallon Zip-loc bag, combine the first six dry ingredients. Shake the bag until the ingredients are well combined. Set aside.

5. In a large mixing bowl, place the brown sugar, vegan cane sugar, flax-gel mix, oil, and applesauce. Whisk until well combined.

6. Add the dry ingredient mixture in the bag to the mixing bowl. Using a spatula, blend until combined. The dough will be slightly sticky.

7. Using a standard cookie scoop (about 2 level Tbsps), scoop up the dough and place on the prepared cookie sheets. Using the back of a fork, press cookies to about ½ inch thickness.

8. Bake for 12 to 14 minutes until spread out and golden in color.

9. Remove from the oven and allow the cookies to cool completely on the pan. Cookies will appear soft when taken out of the oven but will harden as they cool.  Enjoy!

# STRAWBERRY OATMEAL JAM BARS

**Yields about 9 large bars**

## Ingredients:

Dry:

1 ½  C Infamous 8 flour blend

1 ½  C organic gluten-free old fashion oats

1  tsp baking powder

½ tsp organic sea salt

1  tsp organic ground cinnamon

½ C organic brown sugar

½ C vegan cane sugar

Wet:

¾ C soy-free **Earth Balance** butter spread

2 Tbsps organic unsweetened applesauce

¼ C organic strawberry jam

1 ½ C organic fresh strawberries, sliced lengthwise

## Directions:

1  Preheat oven to 350F.

2  Line an 8 x 8-inch square baking pan with parchment paper. Set aside.

3  In a large mixing bowl, place all of the dry ingredients.

4  Add the butter spread and applesauce. Mix by hand until the dough resembles coarse crumbs.

5  Make the crust by pressing half of the dough firmly into the bottom of the baking pan, and pressing it all the way into the corners.

6  Spread the jam over the crust from corner to corner.

7  Place the sliced strawberries over the jam.

8  Sprinkle the remaining dough over the strawberries from corner to corner. Press down lightly with the back of a spoon.

9  Bake for 40 to 45 minutes, or until topping is a light, golden-brown.

10  Cool on counter for one hour. Cool in refrigerator for an addtional hour before cutting and serving. NOTE: These bars may also be served warm.

# CHOCOLATE CHIP COOKIES

**Difficulty**

**Yields about 32 cookies**

## Ingredients:

3 C Infamous 8 flour blend

1 tsp organic sea salt

1 tsp baking soda

1 C soy-free **Earth Balance** buttery spread

1 C organic brown sugar

¼ C vegan cane sugar

2 organic pasture-raised eggs (*see notes for egg-free variations)

1 tsp gluten-free organic vanilla extract

2 C **Enjoy Life** mini chocolate chips

## Directions:

**1** Preheat oven to 350F.

**2** Line two cookie sheets with parchment paper. Set aside.

**3** In a large bowl, combine the first three ingredients.

**4** In a second large bowl, add the buttery spread, brown sugar, and vegan cane sugar. Using an electric mixer, cream at medium speed until fluffy.

**5** With the mixer running, beat in the eggs and vanilla extract until well combined. Turn off the mixer.

**6** Using a wooden spoon, slowly incorporate the flour mixture into the creamed mixture.

**7** Add the mini chocolate chips, and stir gently to distribute them throughout the dough.

**8** Using a cookie scoop (or 2 level Tbsps of dough if you do not have a scoop), form the cookies and place on the prepared cookie sheets, leaving room between cookies for them to spread. For *egg-free variation, you must press cookies to about 1/2 inch thickness using the back of a fork.

**9** Bake for 10 to 12 minutes or until light golden brown. Cool cookies on the pan. Enjoy. Store the cookies in an airtight container.

***Egg free variation:** In a small cup, combine 2 Tbsps of golden flaxmeal and 4 Tbsps of warm water. Let sit for 5 minutes, or until it forms a gel-like consistency. Follow same steps as above but use the flax-gel instead of the eggs. After mixing in chocolate chips, add 2 Tbsps of warm water to the mixture. Then continue to step 8. This may yield fewer cookies.

# CHOCOLATE MOUSSE CAKE w/chocolate ganache

**Yields one, two-layer cake/ 8 – 10 servings**

## Ingredients:

Dry:

2 C Infamous 8 flour blend

⅔ C unsweetened organic cocoa powder

1 C vegan cane sugar

2 tsp baking powder

1 tsp baking soda

1 tsp organic sea salt

Wet:

1 C coconut milk or (non-dairy) milk of your choice

½ C organic filtered extra virgin olive oil

8 oz. organic unsweetened applesauce

1 tsp organic gluten-free pure vanilla extract

4 Tbsps hot water

## Directions:

**1** Preheat oven to 350F.

**2** Grease two 8-inch round cake pans with nonstick organic oil spray of choice, then coat the bottom and sides of the pans with unsweetened cocoa powder or the flour blend.

**3** In a large mixing bowl, stir together all of the dry ingredients.

**4** In the same bowl, add the milk, oil, applesauce, vanilla extract, and hot water to the dry mix. Mix by hand using a whisk until the batter is smooth.

**5** Divide evenly between the two prepared cake pans.

**6** Bake for 20 to 25 minutes, or until a toothpick inserted into the center of the cake comes out clean.

**7** Cool the cakes for 15 minutes before removing them from their pans to cool on wire racks.

**8** Once cooled, place the cakes on 10-inch cardboard cake circles, and place in the refrigerator. See suggestions below on how to complete your cake.

**SEE THE NEXT PAGE for the Chocolate Coconut Mousse and Chocolate Ganache Glaze Recipes**

# CHOCOLATE GANACHE

**Difficulty**

**Yields 2 cups**

## Ingredients:

3 C **Enjoy Life** chocolate chips

¾ C coconut milk or (non-dairy) milk of your choice

1 Tbsp gluten-free vanilla extract

## Directions:

**1** In a medium mixing bowl, place the chocolate chips. Set aside.

**2** Place coconut milk in a small saucepan with a sturdy bottom, and at medium temperature, heat the coconut milk until just boiling.

**3** Remove the pan from the stove. Stir in the vanilla extract.

**4** Pour the hot milk mixture over the chocolate chips in the bowl. Whisk until the chips are completely melted and the mixture is smooth.

**5** Allow the ganache glaze to cool for 10 minutes. Set aside 6 Tbsps of ganache for the mousse recipe that follows.

**6** Allow the rest of the ganache to cool to room temperature to thicken. Then it will be ready to pour over the completed layer cake.

# CHOCOLATE COCONUT MOUSSE

**Yields 2 cups**

## Ingredients:

2 cans organic full-fat coconut milk, chilled overnight in refrigerator

2 Tbsps vegan cane sugar

6 Tbsps chocolate ganache *(see ganache recipe page 58)*

## Directions:

**1** Open the cans of coconut milk carefully, making sure the tops are facing up.

**2** Using a metal spoon, scoop out the hardened coconut cream at the top of the cans, and place it in a large mixing bowl. Discard any remaining liquid at the bottom of the cans.

**3** Using an electric hand mixer, slowly whip the coconut cream as if you were whipping regular whipped cream.

**4** With the mixer running, add the vegan cane sugar and chocolate ganache. Whip until fluffy. Don't over-whip.

**5** The mousse should be a spreadable consistency.

# ASSEMBLING the CAKE

**1** Place one of the cake layers on a serving plate.

**2** Spread the chocolate mousse evenly over the top, working your way to the edges but not going over them.

**3** Place the second cake on top of the mousse-covered bottom cake. Press down lightly to even out the mousse and the cake layers, but not so hard that the mousse leaks out of the sides.

**4** Pour the chocolate ganache glaze over the top of the cake, starting at the center and working outward to ensure even coverage down the sides.

**5** Refrigerate the cake for a couple of hours, slice, and serve.

# FUDGE BROWNIES

**Yields about 9 large or 12 small, bite-size brownies**

## Ingredients:

Dry:

½ C organic white rice flour

¼ C organic sorghum flour

¼ C organic tapioca flour

¾ C organic cacao powder

½ tsp organic sea salt

½ tsp baking soda

*1 C vegan cane sugar or coconut palm sugar *(see variations below)*

½ C **Enjoy Life** mini chocolate chips

Wet:

2 organic pasture-raised eggs

(for egg-free, see variations below)

½ C organic filtered extra virgin olive oil

## Directions:

1. Preheat the oven to 350F.

2. Grease an 8 x 8-inch baking pan with nonstick organic olive oil spray, or line the pan with cooking parchment paper or aluminum foil so that all the sides are covered. Set aside.

3. In a large mixing bowl, mix all the dry ingredients except sugar and chocolate chips.

4. In another large mixing bowl, combine the sugar and eggs. Whisk together by hand with until fluffy.

5. Whisk in the oil and continue whisking until the mixture thickens, about 2 minutes.

6. Add the dry ingredients to the wet mixture. Using a wooden spoon, mix by hand about 50 strokes or until smooth.

7. Place brownie mixture in the prepared pan. Spread chocolate chips evenly on top. Bake for 20 to 25 minutes, until firm in the center.

8. Cool in the pan on a wire rack. Cut into one or two inch squares and serve. Enjoy!

## Variations

Coconut palm sugar: For a healthier alternative, replace 1 C of vegan cane sugar for 1 C coconut palm sugar.

Egg-free brownies: Replace 2 eggs with ½ C of organic applesauce. Bake the brownies for an additional 5 to 10 minutes. The total bake time will be 25 to 35 minutes. Make sure they don't burn.

# APPLE CIDER DONUTS

**Difficulty**

**Yields about 12 donuts**

## Ingredients:

Dry:

2 C Infamous 8 flour blend

½ C vegan cane sugar

½ tsp baking powder

½ tsp baking soda

½ tsp organic sea salt

½ tsp organic cinnamon

Wet:

½ C organic unsweetened applesauce

½ C organic apple cider

½ C organic expeller pressed canola oil, or organic unrefined virgin coconut oil, melted
*(organic filtered extra virgin olive oil can be substituted)*

**Cinnamon/Sugar topping**

2 tsp organic cinnamon

6 Tbsps organic sugar

\* 1 Tbsp soy-free, **Earth's Balance** buttery spread melted

## Directions:

**1** Preheat oven to 350F.

**2** Lightly spray two donut pans with nonstick organic oil of choice. Set aside.

**3** In a small bowl, combine cinnamon and sugar only, and set aside for topping.

**4** In a large mixing bowl, place all the dry ingredients.

**5** In a separate bowl, whisk together the applesauce, apple cider, and oil.

**6** Combine the wet ingredients with the dry. Mix with a rubber spatula until well combined. Do not over-mix.

**7** Transfer the dough into a decorator's bag fitted with a large round tip. If you don't have one, use a quart-sized Zip-lock bag. Place the dough in it, close the top end with an elastic band, and cut one corner of the bag.

**8** Pipe a ring of batter into each of the donut molds.

**9** Bake 10 to 14 minutes.

**10** Remove from the oven, and run the tip of a knife around the edge of each donut mold to loosen before flipping the pan over. Place the donuts on a wire rack to cool.

**11** While they are cooling, melt the \*buttery spread in a small, microwave-safe bowl. Heat for 15 seconds or until melted. With a pastry brush, lightly coat each donut with melted buttery spread and immediately dip in cinnamon/sugar topping.

**12** Place on a serving plate, and enjoy.

# EASY PEASY CHOCOLATE CAKE DONUTS

**Yields about 12 donuts**

## Ingredients:

Dry:

1 ¼ C Infamous 8 flour blend

½ C unsweetened organic cacao powder

½ tsp baking powder

½ tsp baking soda

½ tsp organic sea salt

½ C vegan cane sugar

Wet:

½ C organic applesauce

¼ C organic rice milk or (non-dairy) milk of choice

¼ C hot water

½ tsp organic gluten-free vanilla extract

¼ C organic filtered extra virgin olive oil

## Directions:

1  Preheat the oven to 350F.

2  Lightly spray two donut pans with non-stick organic oil of choice. Set aside.

3  Place all dry ingredients in a large mixing bowl. Stir until well combined.

4  Add all wet ingredients to dry ingredients, and mix with a wooden spoon by hand until smooth. Don't over mix.

5  Transfer the mixture into a decorator's bag fitted with a large round tip. If you don't have one, use a quart-sized Zip-lock bag. Fill with the batter. Close off the top with an elastic band. Cut one corner of the bag.

6  Pipe a ring of batter into each of the donut molds, and bake 10 to 12 minutes.

7  Once removed from oven, run a knife tip around edge of each donut mold before flipping the pan and placing the donuts on a wire rack to cool.

*Decorate donuts with powdered sugar, chocolate, or vanilla glaze. See the suggestions on pages 66-67.*

# GLAZE/POWDER IDEAS FOR DONUTS

The chocolate cake donut recipe on previous page is delicious as is, but if you would like to dress up your donuts for special occasions, here are a few suggestions:

# CONFECTIONERS' SUGAR

## Directions:

**1** Place 1 C organic confectioners' sugar into a small bowl.

**2** Dip one chocolate donut into confectioners' sugar.

**3** Shake off any excess, and place the donuts, sugar side up, on a serving platter.

*\* You can also use colored sprinkles for decorating the donuts. (See purveyors list for recommended brand)*

**Glazing Instructions**
The glaze recipes that follow need to be piped onto the top of the donuts using a decorator's bag.

**A Homemade Decorator's Bag**
Don't have a decorator's bag to pipe the glaze? Not a problem! A small small plastic baggy or Zip-lock bag will do the job just fine. Place the glaze in the bag and twist the top to close it off. Squeeze all the glaze down into one corner of the bag, then snip the corner with a sharp pair of scissors. A small hole will make a thin pipe, and a large hole will make a fatter pipe. As you pipe, keep squeezing the glaze down the bag towards the hole until it is all used up.

# CHOCOLATE GLAZE

**Yields 1/2 cup**

## Ingredients

1 C organic confectioners' sugar

2 Tbsps unsweetened cacao powder

2½ Tbsps warm water

## Directions:

**1** Place the confectioners' sugar and cacao powder in a mixing bowl, and mix until well combined.

**2** Add the warm water one tablespoon at a time, and mix until smooth. It should be a pourable, thick consistency. For thicker glaze, add less water.

**3** Place the glaze in a decorator's bag, and decorate your donuts as desired.

# VANILLA GLAZE

**Yields 1/2 cup**

## Ingredients

1 ¼ C organic confectioners' sugar

2 Tbsps warm water

¼ tsp organic vanilla extract

## Directions:

**1** Place the confectioners' sugar in a mixing bowl.

**2** Add the warm water and the vanilla extract. Mix together until smooth. It should a pourable, thick consistency. For thinner glaze, add more water.

**3** Place in a decorator's bag, and decorate the donuts.

*For colored glaze, add a drop or two of your favorite festive natural food color. See purveyors list for more information.*

# CHOCOLATE MOUSSE CUPS

**Yields about 6 - 4 oz. cups**

## Ingredients: for ganache

Yields 2 cups

3 C **Enjoy Life** chocolate chips

¾ C coconut milk or (non-dairy) milk of your choice

2 Tbsps gluten-free vanilla extract

*cont. next page*

## Directions: for ganache

1. In a medium mixing bowl, place the chocolate chips. Set aside.

2. Place coconut milk in a small saucepan with a sturdy bottom, and at medium temperature, heat the coconut milk until just boiling.

3. Remove the pan from the stove. Stir in the vanilla extract.

4. Pour the hot milk mixture over the chocolate chips in the bowl. Whisk until the chips are completely melted and the mixture is smooth.

5. Allow the ganache glaze to cool to room temperature. About 10 to 15 minutes.

## Ingredients: for mousse

4 cans organic full-fat coconut milk chilled overnight in refrigerator.

4 Tbsps vegan cane sugar

2 tsp organic gluten-free vanilla extract

¾ C ganache, room temperature

## Directions: for mousse

1. Open the cans of coconut milk carefully, making sure the tops are facing you.

2. Using a metal spoon, scoop out the hardened coconut cream at the top of the can, and place it in a large mixing bowl. Discard any remaining liquid at the bottom of the can.

3. Using an electric hand mixer, slowly whip the coconut cream as if you were whipping regular whipped cream.

4. With the mixer running, add the vegan cane sugar, vanilla extract, and ganache. Whip until fluffy. Don't over-whip.

## ASSEMBLING MOUSSE CUPS

**Equipment**

6 - ½ C bowls or other attractive serving dishes

A decorator's bag, or homemade one *(see instructions on page 66)*

**Ingredients**

Chocolate mousse recipe (above), divided in half

2 Tbsps chocolate ganache per serving

1. Using 6 - ½ C bowls, spread ¼ C of mousse filling evenly on the bottom.

2. Place 2 Tbsps of chocolate ganache on top of the mousse.

3. Place the rest of the mousse into your decorator's bag or own homemade piping bag.
   Note: If mousse does not stiffen, place in refrigerator for two to three hours before piping.

4. Pipe the rest of the mousse on top of the ganache layer.

5. Refrigerate for a couple of hours, and enjoy.

# QUICK CHOCOLATE CUPCAKES or CAKE

Difficulty

**Yields 24 cupcakes**
**Note: If you would like to make a layer cake, see the recipe that follows.**

## Ingredients:

Dry:

2 C Infamous 8 flour blend

⅔ C unsweetened organic cocoa powder

1 C vegan cane sugar

2 tsp baking powder

1 tsp baking soda

1 tsp organic sea salt

Wet:

1 C coconut milk or (non-dairy) milk of your choice

½ C organic filtered extra virgin olive oil

8 oz. organic unsweetened applesauce

1 tsp organic gluten-free pure vanilla extract

4 Tbsps hot water

## Directions:

1. Preheat the oven to 350F.

2. Line a 12-muffin pan with paper baking cups. Set aside.

3. In a large mixing bowl, stir together all the dry ingredients until combined.

4. In another large bowl, combine all the wet ingredients. Stir until well combined.

5. Using a whisk, add the wet ingredients to the dry, and continue whisking until the batter is smooth.

6. Half-fill each baking cup with batter.

7. Bake for 20 to 25 minutes, or until a toothpick inserted in center of the cupcake comes out clean.

8. Transfer cupcakes to a wire rack to cool.

9. Once cooled, decorate with chocolate fudge frosting *(recipe page 73)* if desired.

## Cake and Frosting Recipes on the Next Page

# CHOCOLATE CAKE

**Yields two cake layers: 8 - 10 servings**

## Ingredients:

Dry:

2 C Infamous 8 flour blend

⅔ C unsweetened organic cocoa powder

1 C vegan cane sugar

2 tsp baking powder

1 tsp baking soda

1 tsp organic sea salt

Wet:

1 C coconut milk or (non-dairy) milk of your choice

½ C organic filtered extra virgin olive oil

8 oz. organic unsweetened applesauce

1 tsp organic gluten-free pure vanilla extract

4 Tbsps hot water

## Directions:

1. Preheat the oven to 350F.

2. Grease two 8-inch round cake pans with nonstick organic oil spray of choice. Then coat bottom and sides of pans with unsweetened cocoa powder or flour. Set aside.

3. In a large mixing bowl, stir together all of the dry ingredients until combined.

4. In another large bowl, combine all the wet ingredients. Stir well until combined.

5. Using a whisk, add the wet ingredients to the dry, and continue whisking until the batter is smooth.

6. Divide the batter evenly between the two prepared pans.

7. Bake for 20 to 25 minutes, or until a toothpick inserted in center of the cake comes out clean.

8. Cool cakes in the pan for 15 minutes, then turn out onto wire racks.

9. Once cooled, place cakes on 10 inch cardboard cake circles. Place in the refrigerator until ready to frost and assemble the cake. *(See next page)*

## ASSEMBLING THE CAKE

**1** Remove the cake layers from the fridge.

**2** Place one on a serving plate. Frost the top with one-third of the frosting, working your way to the edges.

**3** Set the second layer on top. Frost the top with one-third of the frosting.

**4** Frost the sides of the cake with the remaining frosting, dotting it around the edges, then down the sides. Use a knife or a frosting comb to smooth and even-out the sides it if you want an elegant cake for a special occasion.

**5** To decorate, place chocolate shavings or sprinkles on your cake.

# CHOCOLATE FUDGE FROSTING

**Difficulty**

**Yields 3 Cups**

## Ingredients:

Dry:

1 C unsweetened organic cocoa powder

4 C organic confectioners powdered sugar

1 pinch organic sea salt

Wet:

1 C organic soy-free **Earth Balance** spread (softened)

1 C organic non-hydrogenated vegetable shortening (softened)

2 tsp organic gluten-free pure vanilla bean extract

3 Tbsps rice milk or (non-dairy) milk of your choice

## Directions:

**1** Sift all the dry ingredients into a large mixing bowl using a sifter or a fine mesh strainer and a spoon. Stir well to combine. Set aside.

**2** In a separate large mixing bowl, combine all of the wet ingredients.

**3** Using an electric mixer, on medium speed, cream the wet ingredients until smooth.

**4** With the mixer running, gradually beat in the dry ingredients until the frosting is light and fluffy.

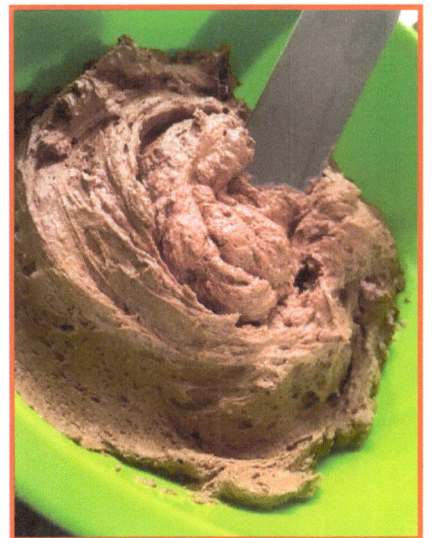

*Variation: For a creamier, lighter frosting, add another tablespoon of milk of choice.*

# HOME-STYLE SALSA

**Yields 3 Cups**

## Ingredients:

5 medium-sized organic tomatoes, diced small

½ C organic red onion, diced finely

⅓ C organic yellow pepper, diced

⅓ C organic red bell pepper, diced

1 Tbsp fresh organic cilantro, diced finely

1 organic garlic clove, peeled and minced

1 tsp organic green jalapeno, diced finely (optional)

The freshly squeezed juice from half an organic lime

1 ½ tsp organic apple cider vinegar

1 tsp organic sea salt

¼ tsp organic ground black pepper

## Directions:

**1** In a large mixing bowl, add all of the ingredients up to the jalapeno, which is optional. Add it if you like spicy food.

**2** Add the lime juice and vinegar. Toss well to combine.

**3** Add salt and pepper to taste. Add more jalapeno if you wish.

**4** Serve with your favorite organic non-GMO tortilla chips.

# MARINARA SAUCE

**Yields 2 Cups**

## Ingredients:

6 large, fresh organic Roma tomatoes, peeled and chopped *(see note below)*

1 organic garlic clove, peeled and minced

1 small organic shallot, diced small

2 large, fresh organic basil leaves

2 Tbsps organic filtered extra virgin olive oil

½ tsp organic sea salt

Dash organic cracked black pepper

## Directions:

**1** In a medium sauté pan, heat the oil over a medium flame.

**2** Add garlic and shallot and cook until slightly translucent, about 2 minutes.

**3** Add chopped tomatoes, salt, and black pepper. Cook tomatoes, stirring and mashing occasionally until they become very soft (about 10 to 12 minutes).

**4** Stir in the fresh basil and remove the sauté pan from the heat.

**5** Allow to cool to room temperature before adding to the top of your pizza *(dough recipe page 77)*.

After you have made your pizza, any remaining sauce can be stored in the refrigerator in an airtight container for up to 3 days.

*Variation: If you would rather your sauce be more smooth than chunky, place the cooled sauce into a blender, and run for 15 to 30 seconds until it reaches desired consistency.*

*\* Note: Tomatoes can be easily peeled by placing them in boiling water for 45 to 60 seconds or until skin splits. Remove them from the boiling water, and set them in an ice bath to stop the cooking. This process will make the skin peel away easily. Once cooled, you can chop the tomatoes, and set them aside until you're ready to add them to the recipe.*

# MARGARITA PIZZA

**Yields 8 Slices**

## Dough recipe
## Ingredients:

½ Tbsp organic non-hydrogenated vegetable shortening (softened)
(for greasing)

¾ C warm water, (105F to 115F)

1 dry packet gluten-free active yeast

1 Tbsp vegan cane sugar

1 Tbsp organic filtered extra virgin olive oil

1 tsp organic apple cider vinegar

2 C Infamous 8 flour blend
(plus 2 Tbsp for dusting)

1 tsp organic sea salt

1 Tbsp baking powder

### Pizza Toppings

¾ C organic marinara sauce (see recipe on page 69)*

1 C non-dairy mozzarella cheese
(I recommended Daiya brand)

2 large organic Roma tomatoes sliced

1 tsp fresh oregano

4 fresh basil leaves, shredded

**\*If you're in a hurry, use your favorite jarred marinara sauce.**

*\*Note: You can add any topping you would like to this pizza, such as onion, peppers, bacon, pepperoni, broccoli, and so on. Be creative and have fun!*

## Directions:

1. Grease a 12-inch pizza pan with the vegetable shortening. Set aside.

2. Place the water in a cup and add the yeast and sugar. Stir well. Let it sit for 10 minutes. After 10 minutes, add oil and vinegar to the yeast mixture.

3. In a large bowl, combine the remaining ingredients. Add the yeast mixture.

4. Dust your hands with flour and knead the dough by hand. If your dough cracks, or seems too dry, add a Tbsp or two of oil and continue kneading. Consistency should be soft and smooth.

5. Place the dough in the prepared pan, and spread out to the edges by pressing with your hands. Dust the top with flour if anything seems sticky.

6. Poke the dough lightly with a fork, so there won't be air pockets. Cover dough with Saran wrap to prevent drying.

7. Place the pan in a warm place. Let the dough rise for 15 to 20 minutes.

8. Preheat the oven to 400F for 5 minutes.

9. Assemble the pizza using the toppings in the order listed to the left. Drizzle the top with a little extra olive oil if you wish.

10. Bake on the bottom rack for 20 to 25 minutes. Cut into 8 slices and enjoy.

# STRAWBERRY CREAMCHEESE DIP

**Difficulty**

**Yields 10 to 12 servings**

## Ingredients:

1 pint of fresh organic strawberries

8 oz. dairy-free cream cheese alternative *(I recommend **Daiya** brand)*

4 – 5 Tbsps vegan cane sugar

2 Tbsps of raw, unfiltered local honey to drizzle on top of strawberries as glaze.

## Directions:

**1** Place the cream cheese alternative in a large mixing bowl.

**2** Using an electric hand mixer start whipping the cream cheese.

**3** Gradually add 4 to 5 tablespoons of vegan cane sugar to cream cheese, and continue to whip until smooth and creamy.

**4** With a spatula, gather the cream cheese mixture from the bowl, and spread it evenly evenly in a 9-inch fluted ceramic or glass pie plate.

**5** Wash strawberries and hull with paring knife.

**6** Using a paring knife, thinly slice the strawberries lengthwise to about 1/4 inch thickness.

**7** Place strawberries on top of cream cheese layer with their points facing in working towards the middle of the pie plate.

**8** Begin placing strawberries on the outer edge of the dish in an overlapping fashion with the tips pointed toward the center. when complete, none of the cream cheese filling should be visible.

**9** When ready to serve, drizzle with the 2 tablespoons of honey.

*\*Note - This recipe should be served and eaten right away. Can be served with gluten-free cinnamon tortilla chips (See recipe on page 81). If you don't have time to make cinnamon tortilla chips then you can always buy and serve with your favorite gluten-free graham crackers (I recommend Enjoy Life Vanilla Honey Grahams).*

# CINNAMON TORTILLA CHIPS

**Yields about 36 chips**

## Ingredients:

6 gluten-free soft tortillas - 9" *(I recommend **Udi's** Brand)*

3 Tbsps vegan cane sugar

1 tsp organic cinnamon

½ C soy-free **Earth Balance** buttery spread, melted

## Directions:

**1** Preheat oven to 350F.

**2** Line two cookie sheets with parchment paper. Set aside.

**3** Slice the tortillas like a pizza into 8 slices to create chips.

**4** In a small mixing bowl combine vegan cane sugar and cinnamon. Set aside.

**5** Melt buttery spread in the microwave using a microwave-safe bowl. Heat for about 30 seconds, or melt butter in a small saucepan on the stove-top.

**6** Using a pastry brush, coat each tortilla with buttery spread.

**7** Sprinkle each tortilla with cinnamon and sugar.

**8** Bake for 8 to 10 minutes or until the chips are crisp.

**9** Let chips cool before serving.

*\*Note: These tortilla can be made the day before, but I prefer to make them the same day they'll be eaten. Serve chips with strawberry cheesecake dip (see recipe page 79).*

# ~ NOTES ~

# Reference and Further Reading

# REFERENCE PAGES

For more information on topics in the Allergy Charts (pages 8-15),
match the numbers in the chart to the links below in each section.

## EGG

Ref #1) http://acaai.org/allergies/types/food-allergies/types-food-allergy/egg-allergy

Ref #2) https://www.cdc.gov/flu/protect/vaccine/egg-allergies.html

Ref #3) https://en.wikipedia.org/wiki/Albumin

Ref #4) https://en.wikipedia.org/wiki/Vitellin

Ref #5) https://en.wikipedia.org/wiki/Egg_allergy

Ref #6) https://en.wikipedia.org/wiki/Simplesse

Ref #7) https://en.wikipedia.org/wiki/Samurai

Ref #8) https://en.wikipedia.org/wiki/Conalbumin

## FISH

Ref #9)　http://acaai.org/allergies/types/food-allergies/types-food-allergy/fish-allergy

Ref #10) http://acaai.org/allergies/types/food-allergies/types-food-allergy/fish-allergy

Ref #11) https://en.wikipedia.org/wiki/Fish_as_food

Ref #12) http://www.businessinsider.com/15-surprising-things-that-contain-animal-products-2014-3

Ref #13) https://www.peta.org/living/food/animal-ingredients-list/

　　　　　　https://www.peta.org/?s=fertilizer=have=fish=products

Ref #14) https://en.wikipedia.org/wiki/Carrageenan

## MILK

Ref #15) https://www.webmd.com/allergies/casein-allergy-overview#1

Ref #16) http://www.nutrientsreview.com/carbs/monosaccharides-galactose.html

Ref # 17) https://en.wikipedia.org/wiki/Beta-lactoglobulin

Ref #18) https://en.m.wikipedia.org/wiki/Lactulose

Ref #19) www.intelligentdental.com

## PEANUT

Ref #20) https://en.wikipedia.org/wiki/Peanut_allergy

Ref #21) http://acaai.org/allergies/types/food-allergies/types-food-allergy/peanut-allergy

Ref #22) https://allergicliving.com/experts/can-i-react-to-the-smell-of-peanutnuts/

# REFERENCE PAGES

## SHELLFISH

Ref #23) https://www.aaaai.org/conditions-and-treatments/library/allergy-library/food-intolerance

Ref #24) https://en.wikipedia.org/wiki/Seafood

Ref #25) https://www.aaaai.org/conditions-and-treatments/library/allergy-library/
shellfish-allergy-can-be-dangerous

## SOY

Ref #26) https://en.wikipedia.org/wiki/Soy_allergy

Ref #27) http://www.webmd.com/allergies/soy-allergy

## TREE NUT

Ref #28) http://acaai.org/allergies/types/food-allergies/types-food-allergy/tree-nut-allergy

Ref #29) http://acaai.org/allergies/types/food-allergies/types-food-allergy/tree-nut-allergy

Ref #30) https://www.fda.gov/forindustry/fdabasicsforindustry/ucm238807.htm

Ref #31) sneezedoctors.com/coconut-fruit-or-nut

## WHEAT

Ref #32) acaai.org/allergies/types/food-allergies/types-food-allergy/wheat-gluten-allergy

Ref #33) http://www.webmd.com/digestive-disorders/celiac-disease/celiac-disease#1

## MISCELLANEOUS

Ref #34) https://www.fda.gov/Food/GuidanceRegulation/GuidanceDocumentsRegulatoryInformation/
Allergens/ucm106890.htm

*Website addresses and information can change over time. These were accurate at the time of publication.*

# ~ PURVEYORS ~

A list of products and companies that provide many of the
items and ingredients found in this book.

**Arrowhead Mills** - gluten-free flours - www.arrowheadmills.com

**Bob's Red Mill** - gluten-free oats, gluten-free flours, xanthan gum, leveners, chia seeds, and golden flaxmeal - www.bobsredmill.com

**Enjoy Life Chocolate Chips** - allergen-free - www.enjoylifefoods.com

**Some great places to shop for the ingredients used in these recipes.**

**Whole Foods Market** - www.wholefoods.com
Their 365 Everyday Value brand is great. Some products that I especially like are:
Vegan cane sugar, organic brown sugar, organic 365 full-fat unsweetened canned coconut milk, and much, much more. Can be purchased through amazon.com also.

**Trader Joe's** - www.trader.joes.com
Full-fat organic unsweetened coconut milk, canned unsweetened organic coconut cream, and many other products used in this book.

**Amazon** - www.amazon.com - A good place to find allergen-free products.

**Thrivemarket** - www.thrivemarket.com - Organic, gluten-free, vegan products and more

**Spectrum** - www.spectrumorganics.com
Organic all-vegetable shortening, organic unrefined extra virgin coconut oil, organic canola oil expeller pressed, organic extra virgin cold pressed filtered oil, golden flaxseed/golden flax meal, and chia seeds.

**So Delicious products** - www.sodeliciousdairyfree.com - Organic unsweetened coconut milk, etc.

**India Tree** - www.indiatree.com - Naturalfood coloring and sprinkles.

**Rice Dream** - www.dreamplantbased.com - Organic Rice Dream rice drink unsweetened.

**Daiya products** - www.daiyafoods.com
Vegan and gluten-free mozzarella, cheddar, and cream cheese.

**Earth Balance products** - www.earthbalancenatural.com
Soy-free Earth Balance buttery spread, etc.

**Wholesome products** - www.wholesomesweet.com
Organic cocnut palm sugar, vegan cane sugar, and organic brown sugar, etc.

**Navitas Organics** - www.navitasorganics.com - Organic cacao powder.

**Udi's** - www.udisglutenfree.com - Gluten-free breads, baked goods, and more.

THE INFAMOUS 8
FISH
BRUTUS
SEA TERROR
SHELLFISH
CALAMITY
PEARL BOMBS
PEANUT
PEANUT THE KID
MILK
LADAIRYA MOO
EGG
SHAMUS MCSCRAMBLER
TREE-NUT
TREE-NUT BANDIT
WHEAT
WHEAT GI
SOY
SID SOY
GOT SOY?
SOY SAUCE
ALLERGEN FREE
THE INFAMOUS 8

**For more information about**
**allergy awareness, holistic health, and healthy living:**

email: anna@foodieqfit.com

web: foodieqfit.com

facebook/foodieqfit

# Eat Well - Live Well
# Heal Your Body With Food

www.ingramcontent.com/pod-product-compliance
Lightning Source LLC
Chambersburg PA
CBHW060805270326
41927CB00002B/54